The Druidic Order of the Pendragon

The teachings and rites of an Ancient Order

The Druidic Order of the Pendragon

The Teachings and Rites of an Ancient Order

edited by
Colin Robertson
With an introduction by
Nick Farrell

THOTH PUBLICATIONS

Copyright © 2004 Thoth Publications

All rights reserved. No reproduction, copy or transmission of this publication may be made without written permission. No paragraph of this publication may be reproduced, copied or transmitted save with written permission or in accordance with the provision of the Copyright Act 1956 (as amended). Any person who does any unauthorised act in relation to this publication may be liable to criminal prosecution and civil claims for damages.

The Moral Rights of the Author have been asserted.

A CIP catalogue record for this book is available from the British Library.

Cover concept by Bob Trubshaw
Additional diagrams by Nick Farrell

Printed and bound in Great Britain

Published by Thoth Publications
Markfield, Leicestershire. LE67 9QB.

ISBN 1 870450 55 8
web address: www.thoth.co.uk
email: enquiries@thoth.co.uk

Contents

Introduction by Nick Farrell   8
Preface by Colin Robertson   15

Chapter 1
The History of the Druidic Order of Pendragon   18

Chapter 2
The First Grade - Measog   25

Chapter 3
The Second Grade - Ovate   97

Chapter 4
The Third Grade - Druid   156

Chapter 5
The Rites   222

To all those Members of the Order
From centuries past
And to All those who are to come

Introduction

I first met 'Colin Robertson' when he was a regular visitor to one of my groups in Loughborough in 1998. Then in his 90's he was unusual from the rest of the group not just because of his advanced age, but also because of his knowledge on the subject of practical pagan magic. In the 'round table' discussions we had over coffee he always had learned answers on everything. I often asked him to take a class on his specialist subject that seemed to be druidic magic but he always modestly refused.

I have met many initiates in my time, but Colin was something very different. He was one of the few people I knew who ever felt plugged into nature. An ardent pagan, God was all around him in a truly pantheistic sense. If asked he would say he worshipped the Sun as the centre of this physical world and the hidden Sun which was behind all things, but you always had the impression that he was dumbing down his real beliefs.

He was a small round man, balding with white tufts of hair that made him look distinctly owl like, particularly after one of the strong Loughborough winds. He was always well dressed with a fondness for tweed jackets and waistcoats. In many ways he was anachronism to the fast food generation; he even spoke in a slow measured way with a broad midlands accent which would have nevertheless been good enough to pass a BBC radio voice test.

Although he looked and acted eternally youthful, he always maintained his distance from the rest of the group and although it was a very public group, sometimes I felt with faint amusement at our pagan rituals. One comment he made was that although it was good that paganism had returned to Albion it had "yet to find its edge".

After he died in May 2001, Colin's son gave me a six-foot stave of white hazel, with some Ogham letters carved on it and a cardboard box of documents. He said that Colin wanted a manuscript in the box to be printed. Colin felt that if his son, as a non-initiate handed the material on, this oath would not be broken and the tradition he had been involved with in the 1930's and 1940's would not die. As part of the deal I would be given the rights if I edited the material for publication.

Intrigued, I opened the box and found a pile of papers and a neatly typed manuscript for a book, in which Colin doing an Israel Regardie and publishing the curriculum, rituals and exercises of a Druidic Order so secret to the best of my knowledge it has not been recorded anywhere before.

The Druidic Order of the Pendragon claims its descent to the pre-Roman times and although it is unlikely to be that old, some of the documentation is dated back to the 1850's.

In reading this material, I could see why Colin felt that the new pagans had lost their edge. His was an order where a form of serious pagan magic was taught that went far above the relaxed holding of pagan festivals. This is nature magic that is "red in tooth and claw" yet has much of the depth of the Hermetic systems of magic.

After studying the material, it is clear that the goal of the order was to help the candidate find the God of All behind Nature. It is intense and entirely different from anything else I have seen.

Colin hoped that publication of the material would spark others to re-constitute the Order again, just as the publication of the Esoteric Order of the Golden Dawn material by Israel Regardie enabled that Order to come into life.

Colin's manuscript is a modern presentation of the original material written in a style which is largely free from archaic speech. According to his history the rituals were re-written in the 1920's by one of the last Merlins to rule the order. The general feeling was that these modernisations empowered the Order rather than watered it down although one of the things that were removed was the last remnants of blood sacrifice from the first grade (the sacrifice of chickens in the other rituals was apparently removed in the late 1880's). Although these things might appear barbaric to modern pagans, one has to remember its place in an order that claimed to be descended from real Druids, who sacrificed animals and the occasional human. Yet, even if it is as old as it claims it seems to have harboured a great love for animals as part of all Nature from the beginning, but considered sacrifice important.

I doubt that there is a single person who could go through the rituals unchanged. The First Grade has parallels with the higher grades of Freemasonry, except there is a certain degree of literalness to them. There are few modern pagans who could face a symbolic three fold death, and be placed in a grave and covered over.

There is much within Celtic tradition and Magic which is explained in this Order. I particularly liked the idea of the Druid's Egg, which classical authors claimed was made by serpents, as being a physical representation of the auric shell around the candidate that was purified by rite and returned to the physical body.

The second grade follows the pattern with the candidates repeating their trip into the underworld to take charge of what they find there and finally in the third grade to meet the Gods behind the planets and to take a deep universal initiation into the stars.

The latter initiation reminded me of Gnostic encounters with the Archons behind the universe. Gnostic and Zoroastrian links with the Druids have been currency in romantic circles for hundreds of years, although none of them provable.

But whatever its roots, this is serious magic and certainly not to be undertaken lightly! This is a complete magical curriculum for anyone who is serious about their pagan magic and wishes to mystically explore Nature in a magical and pantheistic way. For some years the pagan movement (if it has looked anywhere) has looked to variations within various magical systems of the Hermetic tradition, such as the Golden Dawn to provide them. This book gives those who seek it a complete magical system which was specifically designed for those using the Green Ray. Personally I would not attempt it unless I had been initiated into the system, however countless Wiccans use variations of the Golden Dawn's banishing ritual of the pentagram without needing to be initiated into its system so maybe Pendragon could be adapted too.

The regular meetings of the Order, which are detailed in the second part of the book, seem dedicated to using the forces in the land and making sure they flow correctly. There is a certain amount of interaction with the faery kingdoms, although these are not the cute fluffy bunny types so beloved of romantics, instead these are potentially nasty creatures that can and do kill.

This is all interesting stuff and deserves to be studied in its own right. I have to admit that some of the ideas I got from reading the manuscript have found their way into my 'Magical Pathworking' book.

Many people, who have read the draft manuscripts, ask me if I think it is really what it claims to be. Although some research has indicated that there were druid groups operating in Derbyshire at the turn of the 19th century there is no proof that the Druidic Order of Pendragon was among them. The entire system could be a modern forgery by Colin Robertson, but having known the man I find it unlikely. It would be very hard for a literary expert to examine either as the material was supposed to have been edited and modernised at various times in the Order's history.

All I am left with is the content of the Order which, if it is what it says it is, should have developed more or less in isolation from other esoteric groups.

I can detect no influence from the Esoteric Order of the Golden Dawn. Although the method the Order uses for drawing its Sigils is similiar, the reason the Druidic Order have for their use is totally different. But the Golden Dawn took its system of sigil construction from a 15th Century classic the *Three Books of Occult Philosophy* by Agrippa. There are threads of something resembling Theosophy and Spiritualism (or even Eastern Thought) with the use of words like Auras. But the system is remarkably free of Eastern terms or much else from those systems.

There are some superficial similarities to the angel magic of Dr John Dee in that drawing on tablets in a magical book is a central part of the magical system. But the Druids were once again using their book of Amhran for a different reason and there is no mention of angels.

Perhaps some of the biggest clues for the material's authenticity is what it does not mention. A modern pagan writing such a system would be unable to escape conventional pagan conceits, such as the historically inaccurate assumption of Ogham letters being attributed to Trees that was first touted by Robert Graves in his fantasy *The White Goddess*. In the Order there is no Tree alphabet and the Ogham being used is admitted as being a late development. Likewise it does not use the medieval texts such as the *Mabinogion* or the *Book of Invasions* as Celtic theological fact, as many neo-pagan writers have done. Most researchers into this subject would be the first to admit that these legends are only likely to be a shadow of the real thing. Certainly some of the so called Celtic gods that had no esistence before the Middle Ages such as Ceredwin do not make an appearance. The lack of references to such texts may simply be poor scholarship on the part of the Order's founders, but upon closer reading you find that a ghost of that information is in the rituals or teachings and one is left wondering who inspired what. If those legends were a dim reflection of the original Druid teaching, then it is logical that a real Druid Order would not stoop to empower its weaker mythic reflection by repeating it as fact.

There is a total lack of Christian symbolism or references. Sacrifice in the Order is not to repair any relationship between mankind and a god who hates sin, it is done because it moves things up a level. Amhran is not anyone's Son, it is the united reflection of both the Mother and Father aspects of the Universe.

For a 'pagan' order it is also lacking respect for any Gods or Goddesses, who are seen as creations of the created; useful but not deserving of worship. The Druids seemed interested in finding the divinity behind nature rather than looking for just another God to place themselves under.

From the point of view of esoteric history, and proving the Order's validity, it is regrettable that Colin never provided us with the logbooks, accounts, lists of members, or much in the way of original Order material. It is possible that he never had them as he reports that the last Merlin died suddenly in the Blitz of the Second World War and all his documents were burnt along with him.

Alas the historian in me has to admit that the existance of the Order is impossible to prove unless this publication reveals more clues from people who may remember aged relatives participating in such a group. The system is so deep, and so elaborate, it is almost inconceivable that it is the work of one or two people in modern times.

This book was completed a decade before Colin's death, there was a half finished manuscript and some other material which could be edited for publication too. These are 'Missives' which have been written by the various Heads of the Order who had the title of Merlin and other rites which I will be looking to publish in the near future.

In preparing this book there were changes that I had to make as the book's editor. Normally I could send the manuscript back to the writer for corrections and improvements, which was of course impossible in this situation. There were other issues too. Colin was a former civil servant and tended to write in a stilted formal tone. Many of the words he used have a different meaning in a modern idiom and would confuse readers. Although he had managed to bring the original documents into the 20th Century he had not quite made them accessible to the 21st century reader. In some cases re-editing this book has sometimes required the re-writing of whole paragraphs. While this may have caused some of my literary expressions to leak into the text, I should point out that throughout I tried to keep in mind the sound of Colin's voice when I was re-editing so that it did not drift from the original.

On Samhain, a year after Colin's death, a group of us worked the Order's regular monthly ritual on the Derbyshire Downs. The rite was a complete success, but all of us wondered what would have happened if we had been all initiated. Maybe we will try this one day, but in the meantime this book aims to get others to set up groups along this model and maybe Colin's dream of the rites of the Order of Pendragon being practiced worldwide will become a reality.

Nick Farrell
Blagoevgrad Bulgaria 2002

Preface

This book will be read when I am dead, a fact that feels strange to me as the writer. It is as if I were in Tir Andoman (Underworld) already and dictating to you the reader. This work, which I have had the supreme arrogance to edit, tells a tale and provides the heart of the teaching and rituals of a truly ancient and noble magic order, The Druidic Order of Pendragon.

I have chosen to edit the work, to revert some of the teachings as much as possible to modern English. Some of the manuscripts and missives used an archaic language that in the 1930's gave me a headache to read and I know the modern reader might find my style old enough without trying to read manuscripts with where f's were used instead of s.

However I have left a few thee's and thou's still intact which I felt added to the flavour and were easy enough for a modern reader to assimilate. I have also resisted the temptation to change words like man, or mankind with less 'sexist' terms. The Order was extremely enlightened when it came to the recognition of equality between the sexes and advancement was always on the basis of spiritual development and about half the rulers of the Order were women. The need for an allocation of words like humanity to represent mankind would have deeply surprised many of the female members of the Order, who were just as much a product of their age as I am.

I was initiated into the Order in August 1931 by an elderly woman Merlin. There were 20 active in the Order and we met at night on the Derbyshire Downs on an isolated farm. I remember the night was clear and there was a wonderful full moon in the sky. The initiation ceremony was one of the most hair-raising experiences of my life and I walked away from it a changed man.

I laboured within the Order and rose through the various grades culminating in my third, that of Druid, in 1939. Every month on a full moon we would meet either on the farm in Derbyshire or, for most of the winter rites, in the huge house of the Merlin in Loughborough. There was a common sense of spirit amongst us and there were never any disputes. I think it might have been because both Merlins that I served under ruled the Order with an iron rod.

I was ineligible for active service during the War because of a weakness in my lungs caused by childhood TB and continued to work with the Order throughout the war.

All this came to an end with the sudden death of our leader and the burning of all his documents in March 1943. Although we had all the material to perform the rites none of us had the confidence to step into the shoes of the Merlin. We initiated no more members but continued to meet until 1949 when most of the members, who were of an advanced age when I joined, became too unwell to perambulate across farmland in the dead of night carrying ritual equipment.

One by one they died, leaving just two of us andneither of us was in a position to breathe new life into the Order. We carried on its tradition in our lives but were unable to do more.

In May 1979, I was called to the sick bed of the other surviving member, who had, in the process of reviewing his life pending his approaching death, become concerned for the welfare of the Order.

We felt that our oaths prevented us from telling any un-initiated people about the Order or publishing the documents. If our documents were 'found' after our deaths and published we were not acting against the letter of our oath.

Between us we hatched a scheme whereby I, who was now retired, would edit the documents of the Order for publication. He gave me all his material that was far more complete than mine because he was responsible for the instruction of all students in the Order.

Under the plan, I would instruct my son, who was not interested in occult matters, to hand over any documents relating to the matters to a friend who is a publisher. The writer is no fool and will certainly write the manuscript.

Preface

The goal is that someone with some experience will attempt to re-establish the Order based on this material. Perhaps taking it from a defunct intellectual curiosity to a living and breathing Order on the physical plane again. Words on a page cannot do justice to the full impact of the training and rites of the Druidic Order of the Pendragon and I hope that many will start on this truly pagan path.

If anyone wishes to do this I have written a rite of dedication and preparation for the officers of Merlin, Mather, Ather and Amhran, which can be found at the back of this book. It will be important that these four people attempt to contact the soul of this ancient Order before they go much further. Once these officers are appointed they can initiate the person who will be the Merlin of the Temple. Then the others may be initiated.

Remember the work is hard, but as the Order's central motto stated, "Do nothing without Sacrifice".

Hail and farewell and remember me on Samhian.

Colin Robertson

Chapter 1

The History of the Order of Pendragon

The History of the Order was written in at least three stages. Early material was revised and updated in 1843, 1880 and again in 1932. I have updated the information and, to some measure, the language of this paper. In doing so I have not taken any information out but simply removed the more archaic speech that detracts rather than adds to the material presented. Whether one accepts the more mythical basis to the history is up to one's own choice. For myself I could never prove the Order's existence beyond 1765 although I accepted some allegorical evidence, which placed it to the 16th Century; the last Merlin was emphatic that the History of the Order was accurate and I can only assume he had some documents which were never seen by the rest of us. Unfortunately if these ancient papers were ever in existence they were almost certainly destroyed along with their owner during World War Two.

The Druids were an ancient priestly caste that emerged in the country now called England in around 3,500BCE. This caste was divided into three in accordance to the three fold basis of creation; there were the Bards, who merged with and created the music of creation; there were the Priests who oversaw the religious rites and collective worship of the nation and then there were the Pendragons whose power was the serpent force and the energies of the land. The Pendragon caste, which was distinguished by their tattoos of the Twin Serpents on their arms, provided the power for public and secret rituals of the Druids, just as the Priests provided the public interaction and the Bards provided the music.

In the Pendragon caste were three stages of development in accordance to their spiritual gifts and powers. There were the Measog (Acorns), the Ovates (Saplings) and the Druids (Trees). The Measog were to understand the powers of the Physical World, the Ovates added to that an understanding of Celtic Underworld and the Druids the Celestial World.

Each caste had its own Mystery rites and initiations but a single council controlled them. This council was made up of three members of each caste, an Arch-Druid and his or her appointed successor. The Arch-Druid's role was to mediate between the One-that-was-three-that-was-many for the council, and indeed the whole of England.

The combined knowledge of the Druidic ruling class was instrumental in first incorporating the worship of ancestors in long barrows and then replacing it entirely with a system that was dependent on the movement of the Sun, Moon and Stars. It was they who built the stone circles for the combined worship of the different tribes of the country. These circles were aligned towards the Sun, Moon or the Wanderers that were associated to the Gods or Goddesses predominant in each region. All tribes had a circle, whether made of cut logs, living trees or stones. Village priests who were trained by the Priest caste carried out many of the basic rites for the less populated areas. At the four festivals of the year, representatives of each tribe would attend key sites such as Stonehenge and Avebury.

Attendance at each festival was compulsory and even tribes at war were able to attend such events without fear that their rivals would attack them. Indeed the Druids mediated peace between tribes at these occasions keeping the land mostly at peace.

The Druidic system spread throughout Europe in those areas civilised enough to accept its system and became the hallmark of the people known by the Romans as Celts.[1]

After a period of expansion and contact with the Greeks and Romans the Celtic civilisation retreated before the aggressive Roman Empire. The Romans soon realised that although chiefs ruled the Celts they looked to the Druids to provide their spiritual identity. Destroying the Druid priests became a pre-occupation for the Romans although they accepted the actual religion they taught.

At this time the Druid council was divided about how to deal with this threat and was fighting amongst itself. The Arch-Druid was too old and unable to cross the worlds to find the solution to the problem that affected the people. Furthermore he did not wish to appoint a successor, as it meant supporting one of the factions in the council at the expense of the others. For twenty crucial years the council only made the most basic of decisions.

While the Celtic people called for the combined magic of the Druids to protect them from the Romans, the Council was arguing. The issue became critical when Celts from Gaul emigrated to England and Ireland to escape the Roman expansion. The Arch-Druid died and appointed a Priest to be his successor. It was as the old Arch-Druid feared, for the new Arch-Druid immediately broke with tradition and appointed a fellow priest to be his successor giving this caste the majority on the Council. Such an action had never been taken in the past and the response of the Bards and the Pendragons was to withdraw from the Council. The Priests declared them outlaws, claiming that they did not need the Pendragons as theirs contained all the Mysteries.

---

[1] The 1930 document adds the following footnote. "Many school text books say that the Celts migrated into Europe and Britain and displaced the builders of Megaliths. We deny this believing on the evidence of our order that the Celts were always present within Europe and that no migration took place."

Some Pendragons moved to Ireland and others to the area that is now known as Scotland.

The Romans destroyed Continental Druidry and the Priests decided that it was time to magically counter-attack. But lacking the Pendragons they were unable to generate enough power to do more than turn aside a half-hearted attack by Caesar. Later they used magic to arrange Caesar's assassination and believed that the resulting Civil War would mean the end of the Empire. The Priests were wrong and the Romans returned to wipe them out completely. The Priests removed themselves to the sacred Isle of Mona and a belated attempt was made to get the Pendragons and the Bards to return to help work their magic against the Legions. But the request arrived in Ireland too late and although Pendragons did land in Britain, it was only to bury the dead Priests on the Isle of Mona.

A balanced council reconstituted itself in the area of Ireland now known as Tara. What was left of the Druids in England was merged into the Roman religion. After the legions left, the Druids returned and under a Pendragon Arch-Druid attempted to reconstitute the Old Ways in England. They were restricted by the power of the Christian Church which had a foothold in the old Roman Towns and the Council was unable to get a power base. In the fifth Century, the Council was meeting at Camlan and under a Bardic Arch-Druid, called Ambrose, took control of what was left of the Roman Army and used it to create a kingdom that is now called in legend Albion or Logres. Ambrose had some victories against the approaching Saxons but died before resolving the problem. He was replaced by a Pendragon called Uther who was betrayed by the Saxons.

Uther's policy had placed him at odds with the Head of the Pendragon caste, or Merlin. This Merlin was gifted with prophecy and predicted the fall of the Council in England and of Uther himself. He realised that a new successor was necessary to see the Pendragon caste and England through the difficult times ahead. He trained one of his Acolytes, called Artor to rule and when Uther was overthrown he placed him at the head of the Army.

The Arch-Druid at this time was a Bard called Blaise.

Artor and his army were successful and after a time the Kingdom was re-established at a price. Artor realised that Uther had failed because he had been unable to get the support of the Christians. At a crucial battle, he decided to appease them by carrying an image of a local goddess declaring that it was their Goddess the Virgin Mary. Rumours went across the land that the King had converted. The Church did not trust Artor and the King lost considerable non-Christian support. A faction within the Council intrigued against Artor in support of his son Mordrut. In response Artor declared the entire council renegade and banished it to Ireland. Mordrut returned with an army and both father and son were killed in a single battle.

The Council attempted to return, but found that after its intrigues against Artor its power among the people in the country had faltered. Its function was increasingly being taken over by Christian priests. Many Druids, particularly in the Priest caste decided to convert to Christianity, others returned to Ireland. Only the Pendragons and the Bards remained. The Bards carried their mysteries throughout Europe singing it in song and rhyme to those who had the knowledge to hear it. Gradually the song fell silent as the meaning of the words were forgotten and the truth was replaced with sentences that filled a belly in a foreign Lord's house. In Ireland the Christian Church replaced the Druidic council and the Pendragons were particularly persecuted. The Christian leader called St Patrick, while allowing the Priest caste to convert and become priests in the new religion, had a special hatred for the Pendragons who he thought worshipped the Devil in the form of snakes. Patrick ordered that Pendragons should be persecuted until they fled Ireland. Some returned, in secret, to England, Wales and Brittany, but a fear of Christian persecution forced them to remain underground.

The Pendragons progressively lost contact with the other Druid castes, but continued to operate four circles for more than 600 years. These circles were in Sherwood Forest, Leominster, St Nun's and Tintagel.

Most of the St Nun's circle converted to Christianity and in 1176 and set up a religious community. They remained true to their oath and did not disclose the other circles to the authorities.

In 1248 the Leominster circle mysteriously vanished and its members disappeared. The Tintagel circle dissolved through lack of members in 1523. The Sherwood Forest circle moved its operations to the Derbyshire Dales during the reign of Queen Mary. This was out of a fear that members might be identified as Protestants as they met in secret. Derbyshire was less densely populated and the location used for meetings could not be overlooked. It was during this time that the workings and teachings were rendered into English.

Despite a period during the Civil War in which meetings were impossible and risky the Pendragons met for four meetings each year. Training was conducted between the Merlin and the students in separate interviews.

In 1765 the Merlin was aware that much of the oral teaching was being lost and he decided to confine as much as possible of it to paper. This enabled a more regular structure to the Order's teachings. Although the massive task was never totally completed and ironically more teaching was lost because of the Merlin's desire only to write what was in his head rather than teach it.

The rituals were not actually written down until 1780 as there had been a mistaken belief that it had not been required. Each officer was required to teach his or her replacement so that they not only knew the words, but could also perform the complex magics for their role.

However a diary of a Merlin from before the Civil War was found among the Order's archives and this revealed that the rites had been different. It was clear that during the period of the Civil War the rituals had been remembered perfectly by some of the officers who were still living but gaps had occurred because they could not remember the roles of officers who had died. To avoid this problem happening in future a master copy of the rite was written incorporating and restoring as much of the missing information that was found in the diary.

In 1880 the Master Ritual and the teachings were placed into a more modern language to enable a more detailed study. At the same time the requirement for animal sacrifice was also removed as being no longer appropriate for the modern age.

The fortunes of the Order waxed and waned for some 40 years. It survived the Great War simply because its membership at that time was small and made up of elderly men and women who were not affected by the war.

A visionary Merlin recruited younger members in the 1930's. Had he lived, he would have brought the Order to some considerable prominence by giving it a public face. The Order had debated such a role but had discounted it because they did not wish to be identified with the modern Druids who were not so magical in their outlook. If the Order's magical beliefs were revealed there was a fear of legal prosecution under the Witchcraft Act.

However the Merlin was killed during the Second World War and the archives of the Order were destroyed with him. No one in the Order felt they had the authority or the ability to replace him. As a result there was no authority to make new members of the caste and the Order had no right to initiate. We lost other members to the War and our membership dwindled further until it did not have enough officers to fill the roles.

The last meeting of the Order was August 4, 1965 and there were only five of us. However we did not close the Circle, as we believed that one would come to rescue the Order and to reactivate its long history. This did not happen and as a result the rituals are being published in the hope that someone will do just that.

Chapter 2

The First Grade - Measog

Upon their initiation each Druid was given a collection of documents, which they had to copy by hand and then memorise. Once they were committed to memory the copies had to be destroyed. I had of course destroyed all mine, but before he died a member of the Order who was Guardian of the Manuscripts gave me a complete set. The teaching covers the rites (which I have placed in a separate section), the explanation of the rites, the myth, which is the basis of the Magical system of the Pendragons, and miscellaneous teaching that was considered important.

In the second grade this material was developed and it was done so again in the Third grade. In the first grade one performed basic rites and meditation, this developed until the person was capable of working complex rites. Once this stage was achieved then the person started to acquire the sorts of powers attributed to the Ancient Druids. In my experience these started to spontaneously appear in the person from the outset of their initiation. With each gift came more responsibly and more tasks for them to do, it was as if Amhran (The

Song) needed more magically aware people to show more to the Spark within them. For this reason many of us had periods of our lives, which would have crushed many. However as we were given the powers to deal with such moments we seemed better able to cope.

The Mystery of the Creation of the World

Oinacos (One United) created Three but the Three were of its blood. The first of the Three was the Ather (Father) who was built of Light and the second was the Mather (Mother) who was of Night. The last was Amhran (The Song), which joined the two in harmony.

The Oinacos wished to know what it was and it asked the Ather.

"You are the Light," said the Ather.

The Oinacos asked the Mather.

"You are Dark," said the Mather.

The Oinacos asked Amhran.

"I will show you," said Amhran and he built a circle of fire about him and turned himself into the sky. All around was darkness but pricked with starlight so that everything was perfectly in balance. Amhran sang of the Universe and how all was the Oinacos.

The Oinacos wanted to know how it created and it asked the Ather.

"You create with the Red Pendragon of Fire," said the Ather.

The Oinacos asked the Mather.

"You create with the White Pendragon of Water," said the Mather.

The Oinacos asked Amhran.

"I will show you," said Amhran and he took the Red Pendragon of Fire and the White Pendragon of Water and wound them around his arms. Holding them on high he created the first Breath and then the first Stone. Then he did sing of how the Oinacos created Breath and Stone from Fire and Water.

The Oinacos wished to know why he created all these things and he asked the Ather.

The First grade - Measog

"Because it is your nature to Create," said the Ather.

Then the Oinacos asked the Mather.

"Because you need create so that you have something to contain and break down," said the Mather.

Then the Oinacos asked Amhran.

"I will show you," said Amhran. He created an egg of fire and within it he placed the seed of the Ather, which glowed, white and warm in its breast. He took the dark egg of the Mather and placed it so that it reflected the light of the seed of the Ather. And the seed of the Ather entered the egg of the Mather and a fusion of them both appeared called the Earth. The Mather loved the Earth her daughter and circled about her and the Earth loved her Ather and circled around him.

The seed of the Ather became the Sun and he sang the note of Solar Wisdom, the egg of the Mather became the Moon and she sang the note of Lunar Wisdom. But the Earth sang no song for it was not her time to do so.

Then Amhran played five more notes on his harp and the five Wanderers were born and their notes were added to Amhran of the universe. But still the Earth sang no song, for it was not her time to do so.

Then Amhran played his harp and lo on the Earth creatures were created. First upon the rock grew moss, from the moss grew the oak, and from the oak grew the Mistletoe. Then grew the other six Trees of the Primal Song. But the trees were dead and the creatures of the earth but corpses frozen in time and still the Earth sung no song for it was not her time to do so.

Then Amhran struck all seven strings of his harp and the Sun, the Moon and the Wanderers all began to sing. Amhran raised his arms and moved the four elements and there was created the image of a Man. But it was lifeless. Then Amhran divided the man into two and enabled one to reflect the Mather and the other to reflect the Ather. But still they were dead corpses frozen in time and the Earth sung no song for it was not her time to do so.

Then Amhran realised that to show the Oinacos why he created, creation needed to be as vibrant as the Three that were One. And Amhran went to the Mather and said "Kill me that I may enter into creation."

And the Mather placed him in a Cauldron, sealed it and cooked Amhran for three days and three nights. But when she opened the lid, Amhran flew upwards like a cloud and approached the Ather.

"Kill me that I may enter into creation," said Amhran.

And the Ather struck him with lightning until there was not even a cloud left. But as a spirit Amhran rose upward to approach the Oinacos.

"Kill me that I may enter into creation," said Amhran.

"Why would I want to do such a thing," asked the Oinacos.

"That you may see your face in all creation as if you were looking in a clear pool of still water," said Amhran.

And the Oinacos cut off Amhran's head and his blood poured onto creation. And the Oinacos said: "Dying is to live in your creation, for nothing is achieved without a sacrifice go forth then and dwell within your creation."

And lo Amhran dwelt in every thing and all was alive, rock, tree, animal and man. But still the Earth did not sing for it was not her time to do so.

And Amhran cried forth from within creation to the Oinacos. "I have failed! I wished to hold thee up a mirror that you would understand thyself utterly."

And the Oinacos looked upon Amhran's work and found it a Song of Praise rather than a Tale of Truth.

"Amhran," said he. "Name the highest beings in your creation."

"Mankind," said Amhran. "For they are born of the seven notes of creation and my own being."

"Very well," said the Oinacos. "I shall send my spirit into Mankind and I will learn of Myself through your creation. But for me to understand myself completely in your creation I must bring about a change."

And with that he struck Amhran's harp with such discord that the whole of creation shook and thus was evil and unbalance created.

Only then did the Oinacos enter into Amhran's creation and the World sung, for it was her time.

On the Mystery of Creation [2]

Oh Druid of the First grade. This legend is one of the most ancient and excellent allegories. It was told in legend so that even the most base could remember and carry it through the rest of their training. In it are contained many secret teachings which may be found in profound meditation.

This is not the sort of base level meditation for the secrets, which it will provide, can only be found if the meditation is carried out in Nature. Its subtlety and profundity will be best revealed if such meditations are carried out an hour before and after dawn during Spring. You must hear the Amhran as it moves in creation and when the silence of Winter is broken by the first buds of Spring. Then the Song is easier to hear.

Know this, that the Myth of Creation describes all things as a reflection of Oinacos. These include the Mather, Ather and Amhran. All things are a division that looks towards the Total. We hear Amhran in creation but we also see the Mather, Ather and the Oinacos.

Amhran must undergo a three-fold death in which to manifest in creation, for nothing can be created without sacrifice. We have such a three-fold death in the first-degree rite and this is to remind the divine aspect of the Oinacos to hear Amhran and start to live its destiny on Earth.

The Red Pendragon of the Mather and the White Pendragon of the Ather are here used to control the elemental nature of the Earth. Notice that the position that Amhran stands in when he uses them. They are identical to the position of creation taught to you in the first-degree initiation. The red and the white rope that is given to you in this degree symbolises your ability to control the elements and the creatures associated with them. The Red and the White Pendragons are also used in the Wand of the Merlin to build the Ubh of the aspirant into a more perfected form. Meditation on these symbols will yield much.

---

[2] These notes were found in various documents and were written by different Merlins during the Order's History.

Think not as of the Amhran, the Mather, Ather and the Oinacos as simply Gods, they are but one God in different aspects. Oinacos is in the Ancient tongue One Thing or One Uniting while Ather means Father, Mather means Mother and Amhran means Song. They are God performing different functions, which, for convenience sake, we name just as we would name gas as a light or as a fire depending on its use.

Of music in the Mystery of Creation

There are those who say that our teachings in this order derive from the Greek philosopher Pythagoras or indeed the Mysteries of Orpheus. However we can say emphatically that our Ancient and Mysterious Order predates many of these esteemed sources and may even have been the source of inspiration unto them. Although our teachings have remained publicly secret we have, on occasion, met with initiates of other mysteries from time to time.

For an oath taken in secret is binding across orders so much as the teachings are never allowed to fall among the profane. That the seven stringed lyre was known unto the Celts is aptly documented and according to our tradition it was used for millennia before the Greeks and the Romans placed our people under the yoke of this name.

Of the Invisible Parts of the Body

Each person has about them an Ubh [egg] of fire that surroundeth them. Its boundaries extend at will and can merge with the fire of others. This fire, which is like unto the fire of the Ather that encompasseth the whole of creation, giveth birth to the physical form within. It is like unto an egg in shape and in nature with its natural top being a cubit above the head of a man. It acteth as a cauldron for all the life force of the Man and it containeth his intellect and emotions and memories for each lifetime. The Ubh of a Druid is called the Beitherebh or serpent's egg because after thy three-fold-death thou art given a new sheath of fire created by the Pendragon force.

A handspan from the Ubh of Fire is the Ubhmather [egg of the Mother] which is a protective sac that encloseth the rest of the self. Within it are the fluidic forces that enable the invisible parts to function.

The next part of the body, like a yolk centred around the breast and head is the Ubhamhran [egg of the Song] which containeth a Man's portion of the Song including all his memories from previous lives, and within that is the Spark of the Oinacos. Upon a man's death the Ubh of fire withdraws from the body leaving it to rot and that dwelleth in Tir Andoman until the end of the Song. The Ubhmather, Ubhamhran and the Oinacos withdraw unto Mag Mor where it is decided whether it is meet to create another life along the same theme. If this is so then the sac descendeth into Tir Andoman where a new Ubh of Fire is created in the Emerald Heart of the World. Then the Mather attaches a thread of the Ubhmather to a babe forming in the womb that beareth the right characteristics to the will of the Amhran. If such a babe is unavailable then the sac waits in Tir Andoman, if no sac is available while the babe is in the womb then it dieth either before birth or soon after.

The sac and Ubh of Fire is present during the birth, but the process of attaching itself to the growing babe is long. At any time the sac with the Ubh of Fire may withdraw from the babe upon finding that the circumstances of its new life may prevent it fulfilling the new conditions of the Song. This is more likely at childhood as the kingdom of the growing babe may change by random fortune that changeth the condition of its life dramatically. A person of age suffers least from this although there is a possibility that later in life they may have fulfilled the purpose of the Song and chose to depart.

On the Mystery of the Creation of Nature, Spirits and Gods

As his essence travelled over the Earth, Amhran became more complex and individual reflecting its severance from the original source. Tree forgot that it was part of Amhran and simply concentrated on the note it made in the wider song. However it realised that Trees of similar species played the same note and after a time they agreed amongst themselves that they must have a spirit overlooking them. They donated some of their essence to the creation of this Spirit and thus their part of Amhran became a God to them. These made contact with the Notes of the Planet that represented them but were unable to develop further because they lacked the balance of humanity.

Elements such as stone likewise became aware of Amhran at its breast and concentrations of it were large enough that these too were able to generate a Spirit. Thus hills and mountains developed Spirits. In the case of Water, springs and rivers developed a Spirit as did the Ocean. The spirits of the rivers and springs worship the Ocean as if it were a God.

Fire and air form spirits of their own. They are formed in the heart of fires or in the centre of storms. They are short of life but immensely powerful and should be controlled with care.

Some spirits reflected the discord of Oinacos and became evil while others were more influenced by Amhran and are therefore Good.

The spirit in humans however was different. The Oinacos in them forgot its infinite source and often slept. When the Oinacos slept Amhran attempted to wake it by showing glimpses of its own reflection in Nature. However the spark of the Oinacos instead saw power as something separate from itself and worshipped it. In doing so each human gave part of its essence and part of Amhran to the creation of a God or Goddess.

These Gods or Goddesses became aware and individual and took the powers from the Wanderers that were appropriate to their nature. The powers that they were given by humans were their virtues and the discord that was inherent in their natures likewise. Some of these Gods and Goddesses were initially elemental spirits that resided in rivers or trees but the devotion of humanity imparted them with the powers and status of Gods.

But such Gods and Goddesses are ephemeral and are born and die along with the faith of their believers. Some even change their nature in accordance to the beliefs of their worshippers. But this matters not as they have a reality and are a veil for the Oinacos. The Druids of old decided it was better to play priests and priestesses for such Gods and Goddesses and ally themselves with their powers rather than attempt to stand against them.[3]

When a God or Goddess dies, and does not adapt to new ways, it withdraws to the Underworld where it is still remembered by the ghosts of the Ancient Ones. Unless their worship is re-established on the Middle Earth there they will remain until the Singer finishes Amhran and writes the final verse to end the Mirror.

Of the Earth and the Three Worlds

Now the world is divided into three worlds. The first is the World of Amhran or the Earth, sometimes called Bith or the Middle Earth. The Second is the World of the Mather, or the Underworld or Tir Andoman and the last is the World of the Ather or Overworld or Mag Mor.

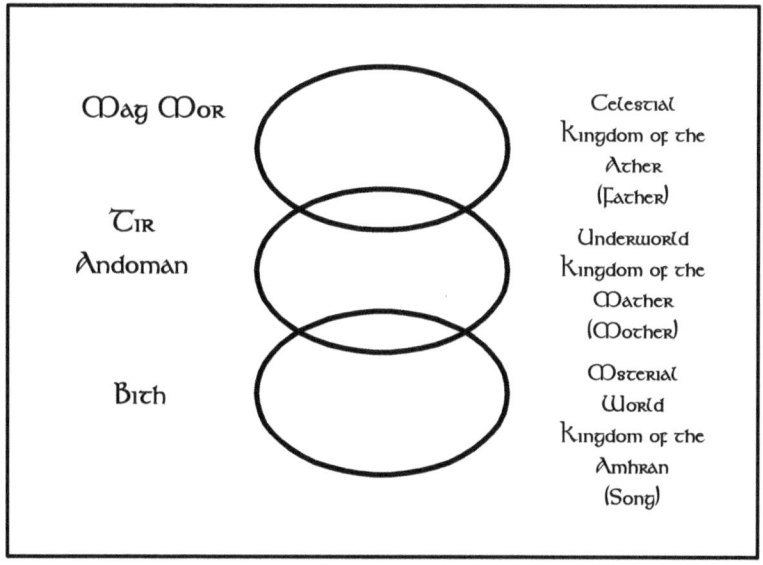

Tir Andoman is visited by death, or in trance, or by invitation from one of the creatures that dwell there. Mag Mor, or Over World, is visited through the Tir Andoman or through certain high points such as mountains and sacred hills.

---

[3] My teacher believed that it was for this reason that Druids of all ages, the most notable being Artor, have attempted to reach some sort of agreement with Christianity and even volunteer to be the religion's priests.

These worlds overlap at certain points and Druids use these as doors. Tir Andoman is the most accessible but is dangerous for it is the dwelling of the Ancestors, Elves and Monsters.

In the legend of creation the Earth is depicted as being loved by the Mather and yet in love with the Ather. On one level this shows the Earth rotating around the Sun and the Moon rotating about the Earth. It also shows the relationship of the Earth to the active and passive parts of God. It is passive to the Mather and active towards the Ather. Thus life aspires to the Light of the Sun and is influenced by the Light of the Moon. Plants follow this position. Many turn their flowers and leaves towards the sun while at night they absorb the moon's influence. Lunar rites are therefore passive, waiting on the Mather to inspire us while the Solar rites are those that reach out for the Ather.

The Earth is a creature of Amhran but does not sing until the Oinacos dwells within her. This is not just because mankind is the crown of creation, it is because, with the Oinacos incarnate in the world, the Earth is a true reflection of all of creation. The Earth has to be pregnant with the totality of the infinite which is neither male nor female nor even a harmony of the two. It is this Oinacos that we are searching for in the mysteries of Druidism.

Of the Nature of the Earth

Our magic looks for its source in the Emerald Heart of the Earth, the action and reaction of the twin Pendragons. It uses this force to control the nature of the material world around us. But what is this matter?

Our Order holds that that everything is made of a substance called Amhran or the Song. This Amhran expresses itself in four types of matter, earth, water, air and fire, which are called elements.

In other words there is one primal force that manifested in four separate states. There was Earth, Water, Air, and Fire. Each element has a quality. Fire is hot and dry, Water, cold and wet, Earth, cold and dry and Air, hot and wet.

Each material object contains aspects of some of these elements. Wine is 'water' as its primary element but because of its red colour and tendency to burn slightly on the tongue has fiery aspects. When trying to establish what elements are present in an object, it is important to see it as an individual. Say, for example, you were looking at a cliff face; it is made out of a bluish coloured rock and therefore would be earth with a hint of water. Now if you were to chip off a lump of this cliff face that mostly had a rich red iron deposit on it you would say that the rock was fire-earth. Another rock from the same cliff face could be fashioned into a statue of a bird and become air-earth.

The elemental content of a deciduous tree changes according to the seasons. In summer it would be earth, water, and air. In Autumn the water and air element reduces and finally the tree would become nearly entirely earth.

Change is caused by one of the elemental qualities in one object changing those of another. For example when you boil water you are taking the hot and dry nature of fire, applying it to the cold and wet nature of water. Depending on the quantities of fire applied some or all of the water becomes hot and wet creating steam (which is air) the rest of it becomes dry and boils away.

The Elements

Amhran

Amhran is a spiritual substance that encompasses all things. Like its name suggests, it is invisible but all other elements are built from it. In its purest state it is extremely pliable and can change its structure simply. It is also the same material as thought and from it is built the material of a soul. It is the spark of life and in its more spiritual levels are contained the seeds of conscious awareness.

Some have called this matter the æther. At its highest aspects it appears like a White Brilliance of pure spirit.

At its highest levels the Amhran appears changeless while in Bith it is constantly subject to flux. However that is an illusion as even at the deeper levels Amhran is constantly representing itself as a perfect reflection to the One Thing.

When one works magic you tune yourself to the Amhran and it brings about new combinations in the more volatile elements.

Amhran is present in all things and can never be withdrawn (or else the matter that it encompasses would cease to exist).

The Amhran also is changed or tuned by the action of planetary energies or notes. This is important as these energies are elemental — Mars energy, for example is a variant of fire. Thus there is a two-way flow of power from spirit, to matter, and back again. Amhran is at one with the elements and the element's interaction changes God.

Amhran is the Spirit of the World, or the Quintessence which communicates occult powers to every herb, stone, metal and animal.

The magical work of the Druid is to bring the powers of the Amhran close to the surface in objects or their own personality to liberate these virtues.

Fire

Fire is the highest or most senior element. It is radiant and dynamic energy and has the quality of being hot and dry. Light is attributed to fire along with the spiritual concepts of illumination.

There is spiritual fire, which is closest to Amhran, radiant fire, which we call energy, volcanic fire (which is the fire element in the earth's heart and latent fire. Latent fire is present in all objects; it can be made into one of the three other types of fire by chemical or atomic reaction.

Fire makes all things fruitful; it drives out evil and mediates between God, the planets and humanity. This is one of the reasons that candles and other fires are important in magic and worship. They act as a symbolic and actual halfway house between the higher forms of spiritual being. However fire also destroys, sometimes to purify an object to a more spiritual state, by burning away obstructions. It is also the bringer of death in that it removes out-of-date structures so new ones may be built. If unbalanced it can represent the wilful destruction for its own sake, creating a lifeless desert of destruction.

In the human body it represents the heat and energy in the body and in the Ubh.

Air

In the creative order Air follows Fire and is above Water. Because the vocal cords depend on Air for speech, the element is considered an important part of communication. Air is Moist and warm.

The winds are an important part of using this element as each has a particular quality of their own. Notus is the South, Zephyrus the West, Boreas from the North and Eurus from the East.

Notus is warm and sickly and brings rain. He looks like an old man with a white beard and shrouded with mist and surrounded by rain and steam.

Boreas is fierce, cold and loud. But he can also make the air serene and still. He looks like an old half naked man with a blue beard and pale skin. He has a crown of lightning and is surrounded with snow.

Zephyrus is soft, cold and moist. It brings growth to plants and flowers and clouds. He looks like a young adult man with a crown of flowers. He is surrounded with gentle rain clouds. Eurus is watery, and cloudy. He brings rain and looks like a blowing cloud that is surrounded by rain.

In Bith it represents the sky between the earth and sea. In the human body it represents the lungs, breath and speech.

Water

Water is the element of purification and birth. Water is often seen as the 'earthy' equivalent of Amhran in that it has many similar qualities. Often the Tir Andoman is described as being water-like. But Druids are aware that water has the ability to directly affect the Tir Andoman. Rivers and seas actually stir up the lower astral plane making it difficult to travel over. It is harder to magically attack someone across the ocean and ghosts may not cross it.

The element is attributed to memory because it is extremely efficient at holding passive magical power. If water is purified or tuned to a particular force it holds it for sometime. As a result it has an important function in healing. It can also hold dark forces and contaminated water is an efficient tool in black magic.

Untainted water has the power to remove negativity. One of the best things to remove negative influence from an object is to place it in running water for at least 24 hours.

While the previous elements are considered active and masculine, Water is passive and feminine. It has cold and moist qualities.

In the physical earth it represents the oceans and rivers. In the human body it represents the blood and other liquids.

Earth

Earth is the densest of all elements and acts as a foundation for them all. It absorbs all energies including the astrological powers. as it contains the seeds, and seminal virtues of all things, therefore it is said to be animal, vegetable, and mineral. It being made fruitful by the other elements it brings forth all things of itself receives the abundance of all things.

It is the mother of all things, of crystals and metals, which grow in the ground and run through the Earth like its veins. Thus as its life blood, crystals and metals of the Earth are especially receptive to different types of the Notes of the Wanderers.

Like Water, Earth is passive and feminine. It has cold and dry qualities.

In the Earth it represents the landmasses, rocks, crystals, metals. In the human body it represents the weight, the bones and cells.

Establishing the elements in a Region

To understand the elemental composition of an area one should observe the objects that are contained within it over a period of time. After a while thine intuition will telleth thee the primary element and what others might make them up.

Some attributions are on colour, or intellectual knowledge about a species of plant.

Try to 'feel' the element within the object. Allow your mind to go blank, touch the object, and allow a symbol to rise in your mind.

[If I encounter a tree and want to know its elemental nature I can shut my eyes, touch the tree and blank my mind and

allow a symbol to enter my mind. The first image I get is a flaming torch made of damp green wood. From that I could conclude that the tree is predominantly earth with a crown of fire (the flames) and a small amount of air (smoke). Opening my eyes I notice that the bark is reddish and its tastes acidic or fiery. It is winter so the earth element is predominant and there is little in the way of water in the trunk or air for photosynthesis.CR]

Encountering elementals

So far we have been looking at the elements in the state they manifest in the world around us. To help in your work with the elements it is useful to contact them at a slightly deeper level. It will also enhance your conscious awareness of the symbols associated with each element. These are best performed indoors, although there is no reason why they cannot be done outside once you have perfectly understood it.

Firstly paint the different elemental images onto wood or stone so that you have the symbol as bright against the dark background.

Next prepare your sacred space.

Sitting comfortably hold the image before you and stare at it for several minutes until the symbol has a glow around it. Shut your eyes and allow the symbol to appear before you as a doorway. The act of staring at the stone should mean that you see before you a white portal with a black symbol upon it.

Look past the doorway, through the symbol, and a scene will start to materialise. This scene will be a representation in Tir Andoman of the element. Do not step through the portal at this point of your training!

This exercise will give you your first taste of the elemental landscapes.

Look through all four elemental portals in one sitting and do not spend more time in one element than another. Failure to do this will result in you becoming slightly unbalanced towards one element.

Life on Earth

The Order categorises life on earth into five different types — from the most basic to the complex. There is stone life, metals, plant, animal and human. These things are compounds because they are made up of many different elements. Humans possess elements of each of these compound natures, which have been acquired during the process of our evolution.

In the man, who encompasses all the kingdoms there is the lower primitive part, which has close affinities to plants that has primal drives to find an ideal place to live, to breed and to draw nourishment. There is the animalistic part that desires to socialise, to hunt for food and dominate the environment and members of our species and then there is the human side, which contains the urge to observe, to think, to understand, to evolve, and the religious impulse. The stone and the metal kingdoms assist humanity to access deeper powers of the universe.

Stone

The stone kingdom is the backbone for material life. There is no being in the material world that does not have as a part of itself an element of the stone kingdom.

Mineral, or stone life, is the Amhran at its slowest. Each rock is said to have elemental and planetary qualities and in some measure a personality. Each rock has its own part of the Song, which is so slow that each individual rock survives the life span of Bith. Gradually they evolve to the highest exemplars of their 'race'. The Celts recognised their qualities on the psychic level and have actually worshipped some of these stones. Such special stones do change the atmosphere of an environment and are evolved by the intensity of human religious attention.

Stones are close to the Earth element and are heavy and provide bulk. In the human body our stone nature is found within the bones and the silicon-carbon that builds the cell structure.

Stones are good at holding planetary, magnetic and other types of notes and discharging them over a long period of time. It is for this reason that the ancients built stone circles and aligned them to different stars or planets. Not only did these stones capture the Stella influence but they had the power to mirror this on earth.

The massive stone circles of Avebury, in England are tuned to capture the solar and lunar influence and link it with the fiery earth influence where it can be channelled into the invisible pathways throughout the country to promote fertility and harmony. Anyone who has visited this site will know that it is one of those rare places where the different types of energy flow in a complex web of patterns. The stones continue to do this despite the fact that there has been no organised worship at the site since the Romans came.

Some stones are active and others are passive. That does not mean that there are male and female rocks, but that rather the energy contained within them has a positive or negative 'charge'. The effect is to either draw power into it or push it away. This polarity is the secret behind many different stone circles.

Crystals have been called the blood of the stones and this is true of some types of rock like quartz. However crystals are capable of holding considerably more charge than ordinary rock. Therefore they are more useful to Druids. However they contain specialised energy and need to be correctly 'tuned'. Quartz is a good general-purpose crystal and is attributed to the Amhran and can be used effectively as a banishing or invoking stone without much extra work. Other crystals' purpose can be defined by their colour which indicates their planetary note.

Red	Mars
Green	Venus
Rainbow, silver or orange	Mercury
Yellow or Rose	Sun (The Ather)
Blue or Purple	Jupiter
Black or Dark	Saturn
Clear or white	Moon (The Mather)

Crystals take on much of the nature of the element of water — in short a water/ earth compound. This makes sense when you consider that crystals have such power and are good at helping to see into the Tir Andoman.

Metal Kingdom

Like crystals, metals are considered part of the stone kingdom, however they are special. They are attributed to the element of water and are therefore a water-earth compound and have a similar magical structure to crystals. However while crystals and the stone kingdom have a general influence, metals are specifically tuned to the 'old' planets.

Saturn	Lead
Jupiter	Tin
Venus	Copper
Mars	Iron
Moon	Silver
Mercury	Mercury
Sun	Gold

The virtues of these planets radiate from these metals affecting anything made of them or touching them. The spirit of each metal is the same as the spirit behind each planet (we will be looking at planetary spirits and how to contact them later). It is these metals that flow around our bodies communicating the planetary influences subtly to our cells.

Plant Kingdom

The Plant Kingdom includes everything from primitive algae to the most sophisticated tree. Its inhabitants aspire to achieving fairly basic things — light, food, and the ability to reproduce. These basic needs are stamped on all higher forms of life, animal and human. These drives, which are instilled deep within us, are vestiges of our plant evolution. It is the plant within us that drives us to seek comfort, plenty of food, a warm bed, and a mate to share it with.

It is important to realise that plants depend on the stone and mineral kingdoms to provide them with material backing and assist them in assimilating planetary influence.

Each plant has an astrological and planetary attribution, based on their effect of their appearance, elemental nature or the effect of them being taken in remedies.

Plants are mostly under the elemental influence of Water, although they have qualities of the other elements. It is for this reason that some ancient occultists have attributed fish to being plant life (although they clearly manifest some qualities of being animals).

Each plant has its own spirit. This is very much like a human soul and incarnates through many different bodies. Like the stone kingdom, plants are working on their own evolutionary pattern. Like stones the exemplars of their kind have evolved to the extent that they were often worshipped by humanity.

Tree spirits are good and evil.

Unlike the stone kingdom, which tends to look at things with a longer term view, the plant kingdom sees things in a much shorter time frame they are also aware of a concept of death and reincarnate. Just as humans can be self-centred or outright evil, so the same is true of plants. Evil and discord to a plant is not the same as it is to a human. Tree spirits are too slow to injure.

Instinct is an important part of making plant communications and generally it is better to you to approach a plant that you have grown, either in a pot or a garden. Plants recognise the hands of their carer.

Animal

When most people think of humanity's deficits, they usually think of aggressive, power hungry types who will kill, rape, and destroy simply for territory, power or kudos. In actual fact these traits are the negative sides of humanity's animal nature. The animal kingdom, is attributed to the element of fire and seeks to dominate.

Even the most passive have this aggressive fire. They may appear to have it caged, but unless it finds expression elsewhere it will bite them and do others harm.

A man who is so frightened of his animal urges towards violence will dream of blood and war. The man who trains for war giveth his animal self a method of controlled expression.

The need to dominate the environment is a primitive imperative for food and breeding. Much of the way we act is dictated, by our similarities to the animal.

While animal needs are threatened mankind will always be at war. It is the animal nature which senses that one person is a stranger to its group and alienates it. Overcoming these things is part of the work of a human.

Unlike plants, animals are social creatures. They have learnt that for survival it is important to work collectively and over eons they have learnt social patterns for success. These social patterns become more elaborate until they become 'civilisations'.

From our animal natures we have also developed the ability to nurture, to protect our offspring, from which has developed higher things like love and parenthood.

Of Man

A human is the sum total of the stone, plant and animal world. However we have abilities not found within the animal kingdom. Perhaps the most important of these is the ability to think and analyse what we do. To watch and to judge our existence and make changes to our environment. We are unconsciously aware of the Amhran and our Divine self and are ever seeking a way to get back to it. We have the ability to view nature and exist within any of the states we wish to.

Some humans do not get much beyond the plant state. All they seek is a house, the ability to reproduce. Others want more from life, they aspire to achieve, to lead their social circle, to have a name for themselves. They order and control those who tend to drift towards the plant existence and fight off would be challengers. These are humans who choose to live in the animal state. But then there are those who see things differently, they are very rarely understood, their plans are always based on the wider view. They are often artists, the poets, the writers, and the scientists. They shape the destinies of millions and yet often by animal and plant standards they are failures.

Of the Kingdoms of Faery

Amhran had created several other races of intelligent beings that were similar to humans but were not made from all seven notes of the planets. Instead they were made from the elemental power of the Red and the White Serpents. They were not created for the world of Amhran but were meant to populate the Underworld where they would be the eyes and ears of the Oinacos. Since they were creatures made by Amhran they attempted to seek their creator by breaking out of the Underworld where the veil betwixt the worlds was thin. Effected by the Discord they were capable of good and evil but like animals were unable to tell right from wrong through the lack of the Oinacos inside them. As a result they soon came into warfare with humanity who they both feared and envied. The wars were over quickly and the Faery retreated into remote areas.

Occasionally they venture into human contact and are generally hostile unless the human has been their friend in this, or in previous, lives. They have perfect memories, which are as if they had a single memory and can see the previous lives of a human.

They have adopted a form of government similar to humans except they are divided by sex. The female Faery are controlled by a Queen and the males by a King. They meet at Beltane to breed and the rest of the Year remain apart. The form in which they appear can be anything they wish for they are made of the same substance of dreams. Often they can appear extremely beautiful and beguiling, however you should not be fooled by this. They are capable of killing and will often do so in a rush like a swarm of bees. They fear metal especially iron which drains them of their life force.

Careful negotiation, particularly with their ruler, can reap some rewards. They are said to know the whereabouts of buried treasure, can teach magic, and to those who they favour will give gifts of fine quality.

Faery often take the spirits and, more rarely, the bodies of small children and babies. The spirits of the babies are given Elven bodies, which have the nature of Amhran entwined with it. Such babies grow to be walkers betwixt the worlds of Elf and human. They are rarely seen on earth again, but are sometimes guardians of the gates betwixt this world and the next. They do not change form and know right from wrong, but can do either.

Of the Trees of the Primal Song

These are the Trees of the Primal Song. Each answers to the note of the Wanderer to whom it is addressed.

> The first is the Oak which speaketh to Saturn
> The second is the Ash which speaketh to Jupiter
> The third is the Yew which speaketh to Mars
> The fourth is the Fir which speaketh to the Mercury
> The fifth is the Poplar which speaketh to the Venus
> The sixth is the Hazel which speaketh to the Sun
> The seventh the Apple which speaketh to the Moon

Thus each tree contains a virtue that is hidden which, if carefully distilled either by art or magic, can free the note so that it may have a different use. One wishing to bring forth the healing powers of the sun should take the sap of the Hazel to make an infusion. Likewise a healing rite may be attempted with a wand made of hazel in which the afflicted is sprinkled with dew from a leaf of Hazel as the sun is at its zenith.

Of Mistletoe

Mistletoe is considered the most holy of plants as it is said to represent Amhran. It has strong powers to cure animals and if half a leaf is taken in an infusion in a cup of water it can enable second sight.

Upon rare occasions it is seen growing upon or near other trees it could empower the holly with the Wanderers' influence. Thus if it grew on an Oak the Mistletoe leaves would give power to kill or save life. Indeed so powerful was this earth energy that only the Druids were allowed to cut it and then only with gold or silver scythes and with the sacrifice of Bulls.

In these times it is cut during the New Moon, with a blessed scythe by Order members wearing white. He who would cut it would say:-

> *Oh Thou who art Amhran we call thee from thy sleep unto the work of the Oinacos.*

The Mistletoe is collected in a white sack but some should always be left on the tree.

Wine is poured onto the ground as a libation to Amhran and the Tree.

When a tree has had mistletoe grow upon it that is a sign that the tree has been blessed by Amhran because it is close to comprehending its own note. Such trees are easier to communicate with and can provide much wisdom when communed with. Leaves and Wands cut from such a tree will have tremendous power if they are not allowed to touch the earth. When not in use they should be placed in a box.

Of Holly

Another of the most Holy of Plants is the Holly. Although it is not attributed to any particular Wanderer, it is used by members of our Order as a token of sacrifice, and thus also Amhran. This is because of a popular legend in which the Holly tree decided to hold onto its berries until the winter to feed the birds who had braved the cold. Its berries are blood red to symbolise the sacrifice of Amhran and its green leaves in winter are a reminder that Amhran makes all things alive even when all around appears dead.

Of Poetry and Charms

It is not enough simply to experience nature. It is important that you find the words to describe what you have seen. This is not simply so that you can express what you have experienced to others, or even that you will forget what has happened in the passage of time. These words will cause a memory of the experience to be tripped bringing with them a flood of power.

Aptly-chosen words, which are inspired by Sight, contain an essence of that power and when repeated will harken back to that vision. It is true poetry and if repeated as part of a rite gives the Druid great power.

For example when communing with an ancient Oak I found myself in the depths of the Note of the tree. I felt an infinity of Light enclosed within the ticking of time. Red, Green and Blue leaves merged into one, I became an acorn, died and slowly grew into a new Oak tree.

Immediately after this experience I wrote the following verse in my diary to reflect the experience.

> *The ancient clock ticks an infinity of Light*
> *Green, red and blue become Oinacos*
> *Birth, Death, Life blur into a single breath*
> *Which touches the earth and the Heavens.*

This verse is not great Poetry, but each word means something to me and is tuned to the very powerful vision that I had.

The next part of the story was when I had to make a healing potion for a man who was suffering a malady of old age. I had made the tonic using the ancient method (described in the second grade) and when I came to the rite to charge it I used my little verse. When before the potion had sat there inert this time it glowed with the correct note and there were bubbles around the rim. The man made a swift recovery from that particular illness which bothers him no more.

Poems, songs and other works of art can be a portal to the Tir Andoman if these are mirror images of places visited. Once your words have described a portion of the Tir Andoman clearly enough you may speak them to peer into that realm again. The art of a Bard or a true storyteller is to make the veil betwixt this Worlds thinner to enable those in fantasy to see history with all its heroes live again. But the best Bard is the one who has visited the Tir Andoman and seen the Heroes and Heroines where they live out their plays for eternity in the Land where Nothing is Forgotten.

Bards or Druids would 'satirise' a person throughout the kingdom if they fell from grace or treated them badly. This is a very dire punishment for it corrupted the essence of the personality in the Tir Andoman. After a Bard had finished his satirising there would be none in the land who could not think of the person but as their comic image. They would be forever remembered as the Ass eared King, or 'the Mean' and would remain so in the Tir Andoman.

Thus it true of every experience you have during your communions, you should tie them down in a web of words that match them as closely as possible and write them in a charm that will capture it for eternity.

Of the Grove of a Druid

A Measog should plant a seed from each of the Trees of the Primal Song in which to form a grove.

These seeds should be taken from the following places according to the old poem.

> *Choose Oak of the Sun*
> *Choose Fir of the Mountain*
> *Choose Willow of the Streams*
> *Choose Hazel of the Rocks*
> *Choose the Ash of the Shade*
> *Choose the Yew of Resilience*
> *Choose Apple of the Sacred Pool*

In other words the Oak should be in a place always lit by the sun, the fir should be taken from a mountain, the Willow should over look the streams, the Ash should be in a shady area, the Yew should be ancient and the Apple tree should be near a sacred well.

The leaves of the trees in the grove will be used in thy rites and the wood from its branches shall be used in thy wands. They will be thy friends and counsellors and the spirits that shall dwell within them shall assist thee in thy journey.

Take seven cauldrons and place within each the best soil. This should be harvested under the Crescent Moon when the Wanderer is under a good aspect. The earth should lie fallow for a month and any weeds pulled out. Each night the earth should be exposed to the light of the Moon.

Then when the Sun is at his Zenith take each seed and impress the Ogham letter of your name upon it saying:

> *By the Power of the Ather*
> *By the Rays of the Sun*
> *I bind thee and me together*
> *So that Amhran and the Singer*
> *Become One*

At dawn when the Moon is at her slimmest crescent plant the seed into the cauldron.

> *The seed of the Ather is placed*
> *Into the Cauldron of the Mather*
> *Let death and birth commence.*

Place a drop of red wine in the surface of the soil saying;

> *Nothing can be achieved without sacrifice.*

Only water from a sacred spring or river should be used to water the Tree.

On the day that the first shoot appears a simple rite should be worked thus:

Prepare the sacred space

Place the cauldron upon the ground walk from East to South, to West and West to North to East thrice. Upon each passing of the East smite thy staff on the Earth.

Then face towards the East and raise thy hands in the Pendragon and say:

> *Spirits of Aire come forth and strengthen this tree*
> *with thy blessing and virtue*

Face towards the South and raise thy hands in the Pendragon and say:

> *Spirits of Fire come forth and strengthen this tree*
> *with thy blessing and virtue*

Face towards the West and raise thy hands in the Pendragon and say:

> *Spirits of Water come forth and strengthen this*
> *tree with thy blessing and virtue*

Face towards the North and raise thy hands in the Pendragon and say:

> *Spirits of Earth come forth and strengthen this tree*
> *with thy blessing and virtue*

Stand before Cauldron and draw the Sun cross with thy staff. In fantasy[3] see white light descend upon the shoot and say:-

> *The Powers of the Ather empower and strengthen thee.*

Sprinkle three drops of water upon the shoot and say :-

> *The Powers of the Mather empower and strengthen thee.*

Then taking for thy note that of the appropriate Wanderer walk from East to West and West to East chanting the name of the Wanderer in Celtic. Each time thou passeth the East smite the staff on the ground. When thou seeth in fantasy the red and the white serpents emerge from the ground stand with thy right hand where the red serpent emerges and your left where the right hand emerges. Draw them together so that the shoot vibrates with the sacred earth power of Amhran. Tell the plant:-

> *Amhran is within thee, now you may sing with me.*

Walk from East to North, North to South, South to East, three times.

Stand in the form of the Pendragon and say:-

> *I declare this circle unwound and the work done.*

Clap your hands thrice and return the cauldron to its place.

When the plant is ready to be planted in your grove. Perform the rite again until the portion where the Pendragons riseth. Instead say:-

> *Sing with me oh note of Amhran*
> *We are the same blood*
> *For Amhran is our Sap*
> *I am Ather*
> *I am Mather*
> *I was with thee at thy conception*
> *I was with thee when thou first beheld the sun*
> *I offer blood for thee*

---

[3] The modern term for this is visualisation

(Pour wine on the earth)
So that together we may grow strong

Additional Notes on the Grove[4]

There are many of our members who are unable to plant a grove because they do not live in the countryside or plan to move house in the next few years. This is a great pity because it is a tremendously powerful magical tool.

However there is no reason why a miniature grove of seven trees may not be planted indoors or in a small garden in pots. Under such circumstances they need to be carefully tended and upon the death of a member arrangements should be made for their planting outside.

Many of you have complained that it takes many years for a Druid's Grove to reach the sort of size where it may be useful to you. After all it can take up to twenty years for an oak tree to be of a serviceable size. However it is important to realise that these trees represent your development as Druids and they will also represent your enduring magical legacy within the world long after your death. From the moment that the last tree is planted they will perform the task of playing the notes of creation in perfect balance and harmony. Such Groves provide a place of peace not only for those who build them, but the living creatures who are drawn to it.

The Merlin before myself built a wonderful grove on farmland near Loughborough and I visit it often. Although other smaller trees have grown up around it and within its circle it stands as a fitting memorial to her work and is a place I often hear her voice. In fact, an acorn from her oak tree has been planted in my grove. The Farmer was completely in ignorance of the magical reason for her Grove and believed her to be a harmless elderly woman who was keen on protecting the hedgerows. Since she planted her Grove he has even allowed the field next to it to shrink so that the hedgerow has actually grown by several hundred feet.

Many ask what size or shape their grove should be. Nowhere does the Order say, although the term Grove does imply a circle. However semi-circles have also been popular and I have seen a

---

[4] This was written by the last Merlin.

couple of lines in my time. One person insisted that the trees were planted where the planets were at the time which made his grove extremely haphazard!

The question also remains as to what one should do while waiting for the Grove to grow to a useful size. Firstly you should visit it and tend it at least once a month. Commune often with the trees, for you are both their parents AND their children. Nothing will help you more in your life as a Druid as your interaction with Nature and this part of Nature is acutely sympathetic and attuned to you.

Obviously you do not shy off any magical work without using ingredients from your own grove. But you are required to work very closely with your intuition to know which tree would be acceptable. Some trees are deeply affected by the Discord almost as much as humans and should be considered evil. Therefore when you settle on an appropriate tree for your work it is important to form some form of Bond with the Tree first.

I have found that simply talking to the tree is very effective and explaining what you are doing and why. Then asking the tree if it would mind sacrificing some of its leaves or branches for the work. Sometimes you get a very clear NO! in your head. This should be obeyed for we do not make unwilling sacrifices. However sometimes you will get this from several trees. I take this as a sign that Amhran does not wish your rite to proceed at this time (I usually will only ask three Trees before abandoning the project).

Purification of Water for the Purposes of a Rite

Take a bowl of rainwater or water from a sacred spring. Allow the sun to reflect on it and say:-

The Blessing of the Ather is upon the Water.

Allow the full Moon to reflect upon it and say:-

The Blessing of the Mather is upon the Water.

Sing the following letters with the appropriate notes

AOU

Now say:-

The Blessing of Amhran is upon the Water.
With your staff smite the ground and say.

Let the Serpents of Pendragon ARISE

Keep smiting the ground in a regular rhythm until the Serpents arise. Then allow Them to rise up your staff. Point your staff into the cauldron and say:-

With the holy power of the emerald breast of the Earth though art Purified

The Making of Thy staff of Power (Part One)[5]

For thy labour within the guild of which you require membership a staff of office is required to be made. As in this Guild we assign different offices in accordance to their astrological planet we request that this staff has to be made under an election in accordance to thy ruling Wanderer:-

If thou art born under the sign of The Lion, let Hazel be thy timber.
If you were born under the sign of The Scorpion make it of Apple.
If you were born under the sign of The Bull let the Poplar be thine staff.
If you were born under the sign of The Man let it be of Oak.
If you were born under the sign of The Fishes let it be made of Rowan.

---

[5] This document was in two parts. The first was given to the candidates before their initiation. This covered the making of the wand. If the Merlin found the wand acceptable then it was taken from the candidate and re-presented during the initiation. They were then given part two in which to make it a fit channel for the Pendragons. As part one was read by someone who had made no oath, it was couched in obscure language, they were told verbally the part in brackets. Apparently in the early days it was left to be 'found' by the prospective candidate. Part two was performed by the Merlin before the candidate's Initiation however the information was given to the candidate as he or she might be required to make many staves in their lives.

If you were born under the sign of The Twins let it be of Fir.
If thou were born under the sign of The Crab let Elder be thy timber.
If you were born under the sign of The Archer make it of Yew.
If you were born under the sign of The Virgin let the Willow be thine staff.
If you were born under the sign of The Scales let it be of Birch.
If you were born under the sign of The Ram let it be Beech.
If you were born under the sign of The Goat let it be of Ash.

This staff should be cut with a prayer to the God who died for all.

Oh thou who art the Singer and Song
I request this sacrifice in Thy Name
With the Blessing of God Made Manifest in Earth

The Staff should measure thine own unshod height and be as straight as possible. [It should be cut from a living tree at a full moon and permission should be asked from the tree first]

Halfway up a slice must be cut to allow the later inscription of letters. The rest of the staff may be stripped of the bark if you wish.

Part Two

Requirements

Three Oak Leaves bound together on a stick of Oak.
One Cauldron of Rainwater or Water from a Sacred Spring (preferably having had the water purification rite performed on it first).
A lit torch or candle.
Earth preferably from one's own Grove or similar Sacred Site.
The Staff of the Druid.
The Sharp Knife of Iron.

The Rite

Walk about the perimeter of the circle with the torch saying.

> *I create the Ubh of Fire from which all of creation was made.*

Take the Oak leaves and dip them in the Cauldron. Fling the water upon the staff thrice. Say:-

> *The Waters of the Mather purify thee so that thou mayest be a just and fit vehiculum for the Serpents of the Pendragon.*

Place the staff into the Cauldron and say:-

> *Thus the Amhran did create.*

Sing the following letters with the appropriate notes

> *AOU*

In your mind's eye see the circle start to fill with light.
With your staff smite the ground and say.

> *Let the Serpents of Pendragon ARISE!*

Keep smiting the ground in a regular rhythm until the Serpents arise. Then allow Them to rise up the staff.
Cut the Ogham letters of the name of the First and Last letters of the Druid's name into the space half way along the Staff.

> *I seal the Sacred Power of Earth into this staff.*

Chant the letters until in your reverie you see the serpents enter the sacred letters. The Red Serpent will enter the first letter and the White Serpent shall enter the last.
Apply a coat of the wax of the Bee saying as you do so.

> *I seal in the powers of the Emerald Breast of the Earth so that this staff may be a just and fit vehiculum for the Serpents of the Pendragon.*

Of the Consecration of Sacred Earth

Unless specified this rite is to be performed before all else. It setteth aside space meet for worship and preventeth discord and beings of Faery from entering into the rite.

Requirements

Three Oak Leaves bound together on a stick of Oak.
One Cauldron of Rainwater or Water from a Sacred Spring (preferably having had the water purification rite performed on it first).
A lit torch or candle.
Earth preferably from one's own Grove or similar Sacred Site.
The Staff of the Druid.
The Sharp Knife of Iron.

The Rite

Mark out the space to be Purified with the dagger and say:-

No creature from the Tir Andoman may enter this circle without my blessing.

Walk about the perimeter of the circle with the torch saying:-

I create the Ubh of Fire from which all of creation was made

Take the Oak leaves and dip them in the Cauldron. Face East and fling the water towards the East, South, West and North saying:-

The Waters of the Mather purify.

Place the staff into the Cauldron and say:-

Thus the Amhran created.

Sing the following letters with the appropriate notes:-

AOU

In your mind's eye see the circle start to fill with light. With your staff smite the ground and say:-

Let the Serpents of Pendragon ARISE!

Keep smiting the ground in a regular rhythm until the Serpents arise. Then allow Them to rise up your staff. Direct a shaft of Light to the Heavens then to the four quarters then to the Earth. Then say:-

Let there be Harmony without Discord.

Of the Iron Knife

The knife should be of normal manufacture but should carry the Ogham of the first and last letter of your Order name above and below the word AOU.

Hazel of Marlow would be presented thus:

<pre>
     H
    AOU
     M
</pre>

Or:

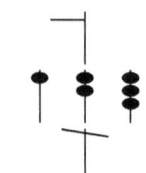

The Knife of Iron is used to protect from the forces of Faery. No faery will advance to within the height of a man of one carrying iron. It drains them of Amhran and thus makes them weak. It is for this reason that they have developed archery using arrows of flint, therefore place not your entire trust in your knife for personal protection.

When an unlooked for encounter with Faery present your knife and draw the following in the air:

The First Grade - Measog

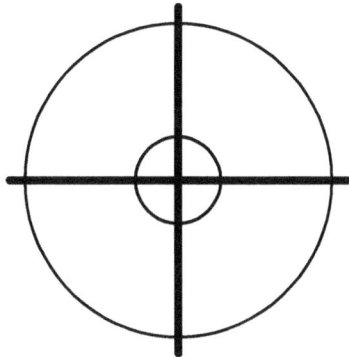

Protection Sign

This will cause the Iron virtue of the knife to extend to some 40 paces. It will not be able to protect thee from Faery arrows which range some 180 paces. It will however mean that the Faery shall flee from the immediate vicinity and give thee time to create thy Circle of Iron.

This is created thus: mark between ten and three and thirty paces from the circle's breast with the knife. This circle should be made with the Sun and will be impervious to faery arrows. It will not offer protection until the circle is complete. Do NOT cut the Earth with the knife, or sink thy weapon into it for this creates Discord, unless there is an immediate sacrifice.

Be wary however of angering the Faery folk. The dagger is only as recourse after all else has failed. For ultimately the goal of the Druid is to strike an accord with such folk to bring forth new Wisdom and Understanding.

Of the Letters

It has been said that Ogham script belonged to the Druids of old. This is a falsehood. Indeed the Ancient Druid Orders made no use of writing until 300BCE when Ogham was developed by the Continental Druids. They saw in it a valuable way of joining many magic powers into a single image. The Britons found it of import for magic implements and it proved especially popular among the Priest caste who used it for mundane tasks and communications.

Among the Pendragon caste its role was purely magical and it allotted 12 letters to represent the Zodiac and seven letters to the Wanderers. It gave each of the letters a special sound and a musical note and thus gave a method of pronouncing and chanting each letter. The Pendragon assigned one Ogham sign so that it had the meaning of Amhran. This differed from the Continental Druids.

After the Priests had cast them out, the Pendragons built three temples, one in Ireland, one in Scotland and the other in the Isle of Man. Each post had its name in Ogham upon it. The outer ring were placed the twelve signs, then came the signs of the Wanderers. In the centre of the Temple, before a fire, was placed a wooden altar upon which was carved the Ogham of Amhran which was depicted thus:

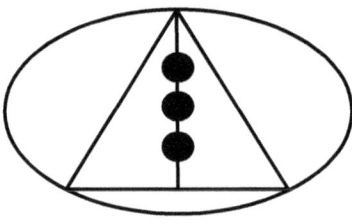

Altar sign

It is said that the Ogham letter of Amhran drew all the notes of the rest of the alphabet together when it was drawn, sung or chanted. There was a rite, similar to what we do today, where a Pendragon stood under each post, empowered it with the Serpents and then chanted the name and note of the Ogham. A song of power, now alas lost to us, would be performed and the result would be the manifestation of the Song of Creation. It is said that healing would come and there would be an end to discord for many months. It was this rite that the Priests wished the Pendragons to perform to prevent the continued advance of the Roman armies. Tradition has it that a similar temple was built in the Midlands and the rite was performed because Pendragon caste wanted to promote peace

The First Grade - Measog

between the Romans and the Celts as they realised that the two traditions were to fuse. They refused to assist in any resistance movements and later became key figures in the Romano-Celtic administration.

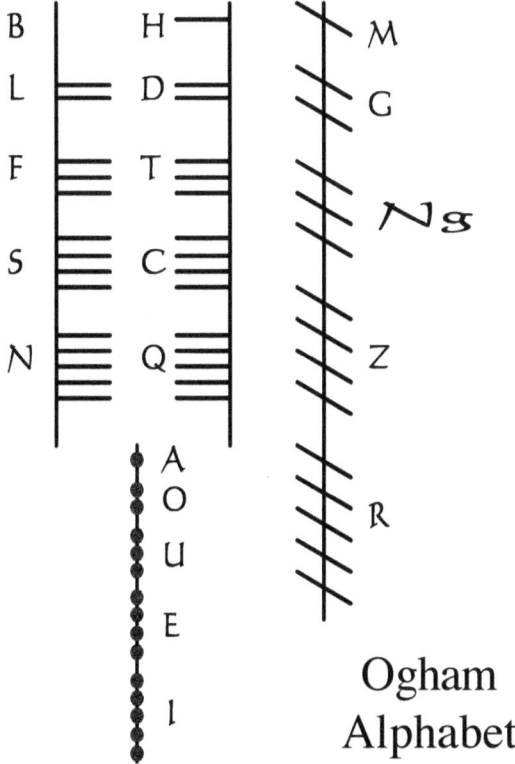

Ogham Alphabet

Study of the runes continued and some of the Druids took their knowledge into the Christian priesthood who attempted to use it to convert other Druids or to contaminate their meeting places. Christians carving Ogham onto the stones to 'convert them' destroyed some of them.

Ogham talismans may be made of a pebble or timber taken from an appropriate tree and then the request written in Ogham upon it. The stick is empowered by drawing up the Red and White Serpents until it radiates with power. The stick or stone stored until thy request becomes true.

Creating a word in Ogham

The creation of a word in the magical script is a simple matter of transliteration letter for letter. However you will note that some modern English letters are missing from this alphabet namely p,w x,k,v,j and y. Generally it is best to avoid using words with these letters in them, however at times this is not possible. In which case c and q replace with k, v and w replace with b, y and j replace with i. x replace with z.

Then draw a vertical line and arrange the letters from top being the start of the word and the bottom being the lowest. In some forms of Ogham the vowels are removed, however because the significance of the vowels within Pendragon druidry we keep them. Some of the later forms of Ogham replaced the circles for vowels with shorter lines this was rejected because it also failed to satisfy the symbolic needs of our rite. These later systems replaced the vertical lines with horizontal ones to satisfy the monks of the time.

Ideally words should be translated into Celtic before transliterating. However after some experiment we have concluded that this makes little difference to the final magic.

Of the Zodiacial and Planetary Associations of the Oghams

Each Ogham letter is attributed to either a Wanderer or zodiacal force. O and U have double meanings - O unto the Ather and the Sun, U unto the Mather and the Moon. A hath no meaning but is instead the force that knitteth them together into the sum total of all.

- A is Amhran
- O is the Ather and attributed to Sun
- U is the Mather and attributed to the Moon
- E is attributed to Mercury
- I is attributed to Venus
- B is attributed to Mars
- H is attributed to Jupiter
- M is attributed to Saturn
- N is attributed to the Lion

F   is attributed to the Scorpion
R   is attributed to the Bull
S   is attributed to the Man
C   is attributed to the Fishes
Z   is attributed to the Twins
Q   is attributed to the Crab
T   is attributed to the Archer
G   is attributed to the Virgin
Ng is attributed to the Scales
L   is attributed to the Ram
D   is attributed to the Goat

On the Musical Notes of the Wanderers and the Amhran

C   is the Note of the Ather and the Sun
D   is the Note of the Mather and the Moon
E   is the Note of Mercury
F   is the Note of Venus
G   is the Note of Mars
A   is the Note of Jupiter
B   is the note of the Saturn
Amhran is represented by playing a C scale

Death

The Druids of Old revealed only one belief of theirs to the Romans. That was that they believed they were immortal and that upon death the soul is immediately born again. This truth was revealed to spark fear into the breasts of the Greeks and Romans who knew that the Celts did not fear death in their wars with them. The Celt believed so much that he would be reborn that he was prepared to loan money to a friend on the assumption that he would be paid back in a life to come.

Death and rebirth are important truths in Druidry and symbolically a death is always followed by a rebirth.

After a man dies he loses his connection with his elemental body, which immediately starts to break down into its material components. In the form of an egg those elements that made up a man's personality along with the part of Amhran which is his lifetime destiny is bound withdraw. The Spark of the Oinacos pass through to the West and into the Underworld, or land of the Mather. There, the person rests and remembers their life and meditates on what has been done and what should have been undone. Then when Amhran and the Spark have learnt all they can from the personality they leave it in the Underworld and then, unencumbered float upwards to the Upper Realms or Land of the Ather. There the Spark looks at that part of Amhran in the context of many lives. If the Spark thinks its work is complete then it will leave Amhran in the Upper Realms and there merge with That Which Sent it Forth. However if it thinks it still has more to learn from that part of Amhran, together they will descend into the Underworld.

There they will be found by the Mather and given a new Personality in accordance to the wishes of Amhran. The Mather will give Amhran the milk of the sacred cow, which causes forgetfulness, and together they will descend into life once more.

One might well ask why if a soul re-incarnates in this fashion, did the Celts enable a debt to pass from one life to another. Like many things this was something that the Roman recorders did not understand properly. The Spark does not forget and Amhran is aware of that which must be done and undone. A debt may not just be of money, it may be of favour or disfavour. These are always repaid in kind even if the person is unaware of it for the act of incurring a debt means that there is something to be done in a future life. If the Spark thinks that it has learned all it needs to from that part of Amhran then Amhran through another aspect of itself, repays all debts.

Of Memory

Amhran remembers everything, the Spark of the Oinacos sees and Understands everything. No man however humble his life, no animal or bird that dies unseen, is ever forgotten. Each part of Nature will be remembered for eternity. Live not to preserve thy name among thy fellows for in time even the most famous shall be forgotten. Instead live thy part of the Great Song and rejoice in it.

Of Sacrifice

Sacrifice was an important part of life in the ancient world and especially to the Druids. We have a statement, oft repeated, that nothing is achieved without sacrifice and in every rite some form of sacrifice is performed. However we have had many questions about the sacrifice of live offerings, perhaps because it is only recently that we have decided to no longer make them.

Firstly blood is considered the part of the body where Amhran is strongest. You only have to place a doctor's stethoscope to the wrist to hear the music of the Blood rushing through the body. The act of spilling blood is the releasing of that Note so that it may be transmuted by sacrifice into the rite itself. The spilling of Amhran's blood in a three-fold sacrifice is a crucial allegory in the Pendragon caste as to how life was created.

In the period of history identified as Celtic, humans also offered themselves to be sacrifices. Sometimes these were criminals who sought to expunge the loss of honour for their crimes in sacrifice. The alternative for these was to be outcast, which would often mean their death, by violence or starvation away from the tribe.

Then there were special sacrifices of men or women who were without any blemish either moral or spiritual. These died in the hope that their sacrifice would bring about well being for the rest of the tribe or even the Nation itself. Such people died the three-fold death literally instead of figuratively as was depicted in the rites of the Priests or the Pendragon caste.

The sacrifice would spend a period of time being trained by a Druid for the work that they must do after the three-fold death. During this period the sacrifice wanted for nothing for while he was being made ready his tribe considered him a god.

When he was ready his tribe handed the sacrifice over to the Druids with great reverence. The Druids, who saw him as the embodiment of Amhran, also treated him with great respect. Before the rite he was given a wheat cake mixed with holly to symbolise death and resurrection. The rite was performed; much like the first-degree initiation other than the sequence was slightly different.

The sacrifice was struck over the head with a hammer, garrotted and then had his throat cut. Each of these 'deaths' provoked a response in the different parts of the Ubh of the sacrifice so that different parts of divinity were freed to be directed by the Will of the sacrifice towards the goals he had been trained for. This act created a sympathetic reaction in the physical body of the sacrifice, making it a divine channel for some types of work. For this reason bodies were placed in the ground where they would be set as Guardians for a tribe, or for a special building. If this were the function of the sacrifice, Druids would be able to communicate with him and seek his advice, for while his body was on earth his spirit was in the lands of the blessed and the Tir Andoman simultaneously. Communication with this spirit was possible via relics that were kept by the Priest caste official responsible for the tribe or village.

Sometimes a sacrifice would not be required to be linked with the earth and it would need a speedy entry into Tir Andoman so that it could quickly fuse its requests with the Power of the Mather before moving on to the Lands of the Blessed to unite with the Ather and thus create the Magic of Amhran. In such cases the sacrifice would have their head cut off. This removed all power that may reside in the body and remove it directly into Tir Andoman.

Celts collected heads as a sign of respect for the warriors they killed and a method of making sure that any earth bound ghosts did not attempt to extract revenge. Ghosts were a problem for tribes where men and women refused to enter Tir Andoman. The body was exhumed and the corpse decapitated and the head placed between the legs. Criminals or foreigners that were killed were decapitated or cremated to prevent a spirit rising.

Among the Priest caste there was also a belief that children or babies made good sacrifices. This practice was discouraged but did happen occasionally, particularly in the early days when the control of the Druid Council was not as strong as in later days. The babies they chose were those who had no identifiable Ather, or showed some abnormality that made them special. The more superstitious lay members of a town or village considered such beings to have been the result of mating with faeries and often would have killed them anyway.

Sacrifice of animals was preferable for general rites. Bulls and cows were used for the most important rites while chickens and doves were used for the more mundane purposes. Sometimes appropriate animals were sacrificed, particularly foxes (which represent mankind), dogs, for health and well being, sheep for healthy flocks and pigs for Other World rites.

I who am old enough to remember when the Order used to sacrifice animals have not missed the practice. I do not believe that the change from blood to wine changed the potency of the rites much. The process was messy and unpleasant particularly among those of us who had a dislike of seeing such things. First we attempted a compromise and engineered a method of using blood bought from the local butchers and later moved to just using wine.

Many of you have asked me if it affected the quality of the work, personally it did not effect mine at all but I was younger then and had yet to experience many of the visions that have lead me to be a Merlin now. At the time many of the older members said that the power levels had reduced slightly, but it made no real difference to the rite. Maybe the sacrifice of such a tradition had created a new and more powerful one for Nothing is Achieved without Sacrifice.

Of Communing with Nature

This paper was considered very important within the Order as it contained the bulk of the practical work performed by the First Degree Druid. Of all the papers that bring about change within the Order it is the Communing which brings about the dramatic realisations about Nature and her relationships to the rest of the world. Once its techniques are mastered there is nothing that is kept secret from you. The paper is similar in content to one that was written in the 17th Century but was rewritten in the twentieth Century probably by the second to last Merlin. The only reason I think this is because she was involved in the Theosophical Movement before joining the Order and there are references to Eastern meditation systems.

Having completed your first-degree initiation you will be aware that the Order performs some dramatic and exciting rites involving many people and paraphernalia. However this is only a small part of the work that you will be required to perform. The majority of your time is spent on your own comprehension of the forces of Nature which you seek to be a part of and to some measure control. In the Mystery of the Creation of the World myth with which you are also presented are contained many occult secrets but the one that concerns us now is how Amhran, which has similarities with the Soul of a person, divides itself throughout creation giving it life. It is saying that every portion of Nature contains a Note of the Great Song of Creation. Part of the goal of Mankind is to see that note.

Mastery of a Note gives a true comprehension of that portion of the Great Song; it is like understanding a subset of that which is infinite. It is humanity's purpose to be the Watcher of Creation and to hear every Note of the Great Song. Then the Spark of the Oinacos is closer to seeing the true reflection of itself and in seeing Knowing Itself.

You will notice that our Myth does not have a perfect or complete Oinacos. Instead the Myth describes an Infinite Being beyond our comprehension, which is evolving by looking at its own reflection in Nature. There is no division betwixt the Ather, Mather, Song and creation, it is just a monologue with a single actor on the stage.

In this Order we use the power of rite to break the mould of our current perceptions and to open the gates within ourselves so that we can accept other views of the world. But the most important part of the Work is to start the process of seeing Amhran in Nature.

The order teaches a unique system of meditation which it calls Communing. This appears to be different from the meditation systems of the East or even the Christian Mystical techniques that aim to move away from Nature. However the experience of these techniques is just as intense, for when we can see God as being as close as our hands and feet then there is no reason to search in the heavens; our heaven is on Earth.

Communing with the Stones

One must find a special stone with which thou findeth easy to communicate. Look for an ancient stone preferably with a religious connection such as the sole survivor of a stone circle, or one that is part of a wall in a church. Firstly test the stone to see if it is positive or negative. Touch it and gather any impressions. Perform the clearing rite in the ancient manner. This will awaken the æther within the stone and give you a chance to communicate with the rock.

Silently project your consciousness into the rock and ask its permission to approach it. If it is the 'right rock' then it will agree. This will not be a voice, it will be a feeling of rightness.

Now open your consciousness further and feel what it is like to be the rock. Next become aware of the rock's consciousness and allow images to rise into your mind. These images are the stone communicating to your unconscious and can tell you practically anything. Some of the first communications are usually mundane introductions and telling of histories. This is important because sometimes you are in a position to help the stone's evolution by providing information that it has not been unable to discover for itself in its stone's eye view of the universe. This could be an interesting intellectual exercise, but its goal is to discover the part of you which is stone.

Communing with Plants

Beforehand prepare the space ritually in the ancient manner. This neutralises any tendency in the plant towards negativity and activates the Amhran in the plant to provide a communications medium. Although plants respond to sound, they have no concept of words and communication is managed by the use of telepathy. Just in the case of approaching the stones, it is vital that you ask the plant for permission to communicate with it. You will receive an instinct if it is a good idea to continue with the experiment, always act on your initial impulse.

Like stones it is always a good idea to put your back to the tree if it is big enough — otherwise touch is usually sufficient. Once again you will receive images which will usually seem, after a while, to be converted into speech.

Once you have communed with an object long enough you should attempt to find its Note.

Holding the consciousness of the object as close to your consciousness as possible hum the scales until you find a note that fits. You will know when you hit it because your depth of perception of the object will expand. You will feel like the rock, or pool, or wind you are working with will suddenly melt into pure consciousness, an infinite life moving in accordance to the one note.

You should make note of any experiences you have in a diary. Now you have worked with the individual elements you are ready to try communing with composite figures such as areas of land or mountains. This is difficult as not only do you have to take into account large amounts of activity, you also have to contact the part of Amhran that oversees the whole area. The Ancients used to regard these Notes of Amhran as Elemental Gods. This is because for that area they represented the over all co-ordinating facility. Contacting these requires you to be standing in the Ubh, or Aura, of the area. If it is a grove of trees, or hedgerow it is best to stand in the heart. Hills or mountains should be experienced either in a cave, or on the top of the highest peak. Streams should be experienced by standing in them (if they are deep enough by floating or standing in them up to your neck).

Like the previous exercises you first relax and communion with the part of the terrain immediately contained within your own Ubh, or aura. Once you have attained this, feel for the over self of that small piece. It is like taking the hand of someone in the dark. You will know when you find it because you will feel a presence as if someone is standing beside you. Ask this consciousness to allow you to see Amhran within it. If it agrees imagine expanding your aura to encompass the area you wish to work with. Mentally say to yourself "My Ubh and the Ubh of [this feature] are One".

Start to feel yourself as being this region, feel the many notes of the different trees, the solidity of the ground, the flowing of any rivers, the animal life within it. Then search for the combined note of the area. This is done by listening to everything and moving through the scales until you find the correct note. It is also helpful to find out the name of the creature that oversees the object. Over time you will develop a relationship with this 'God' and will be able to call it quickly if it will tell you its name.

The relationship is incredibly deep and works two ways. One elderly druid worked so closely with a hill near where he lived for nearly 20 years and felt such a close part of it that he felt as if it were a member of the family. One night he was awoken by its 'God' to rescue a set of badgers from a group of men keen on killing them with dogs. Although quite frail the Old man, assisted by a surprise storm, appeared in their midst quite suddenly and beat them with his staff until they fled. Their dogs also fled and the old Druid believed they lived wild on the hill from that day on.

A Druid who was fleeing from a Witchfinder hid in his grove of trees, which was in a hedgerow near his house. Although the Witchfinder and his cohorts searched the copse thoroughly, they were unable to find their suspect and assumed he had fled the area. However the man had simply sat in the branches of a tree and was so merged in consciousness with the area, the Witchfinder's men had not been able to distinguish him from the trees.

While working in an area in which you have a close relationship, you will find that the trees and even the animals in the area will be more amenable to you. Trees are more likely to volunteer their leaves, branches and bark for your projects and rites performed there will be stronger.

Of Gods and Goddesses

There are those historians who would have the Druids obsessed with the worship of certain Gods or Goddesses. This seems strange to the members of our Order who have, while serving at the altars of many different Gods and Goddesses only acknowledged the three that are One.

Gods and Goddesses are creatures of Amhran born of the sacrifices of men and women who wished them to be. In the early times such people gave power to their ancestors and the Druids acted as mediators between the dead and the living. Later when the people worshipped Gods and Goddesses of sacred sites and composed legends for them, the Druids acted as priests acting as mediators between these forces. One caste of priests specialised in the creation of rites for these beings so that in their worship they did not create discord.

It was the belief in that time that if you failed to honour that part of Amhran then the God or Goddess would cause things to be bad for you. While each God or Goddess was worshipped it was true and the Druids, particularly the Priest Caste made sure that the regular rites were performed to make sure that the Gods were properly looked after or allowed to 'die' in a harmless manner.

Tradition says that people took upon themselves to accept a Patron God or Goddess, which was usually associated with their profession, although there were exceptions. Lugh, whose name meant light, was believed to have all talents.

Traces of what the Druids believed did enter the normal religions, but without the keys of initiation it was impossible for the ordinary people to fully grasp. However in Ireland, England and Gaul the Daghda or 'Good Father' was worshipped, however his actions were but a shadow of what we mean by the Ather. Likewise Bel did have similarities with the Oinacos however there were more dissimilarities. It is possible to see the difference because each God is given a human form and exhibits characteristics as if they were Men. Such behaviour is not part of anything which we describe as the one that is Three.

When the Romans came they categorised these Gods and Goddesses so that there was a degree of order. Those they thought were similar to their own they called after them, they also brought with them the Gods from other parts of the Empire. They built temples of Stone on the sites and otherwise did little to change the way of the people. Many Druids continued to serve in these Temples of their People as they had always done. The Romans did not object, once the Priest caste, which they saw as dangerous, were removed relations with what they perceived as friendly Druids were amicable. Some Roman Gods were also adopted by the Britons and were presided over by Druid Priests. One Pendragon Merlin even became the chief priest in the Temple of the Emperor Hadrian in Colchester.

Early Christianity did not change much in England until the death of Artor. Gradually the Old Gods joined each other in the feasting

Halls of the Tir Andoman, although some were adopted as Saints by the new Religion.

Some legends of the Gods and Goddesses were preserved in the oral tradition of the Bards but gradually these were subverted in time until all that remains of the Bright Ones were faint memories in half-forgotten stories.

But the Druids have never considered it necessary to worship nature forces in order to interact with them. Reaching to the Amhran that resides in Nature one simply experiences it. The awe someone sometimes feels in the presence of a Thunderstorm is not Taranis, it is Amhran of Nature speaking to us. It does not require worship, it requires a spiritual comprehension.

So should a Druid look to the Celts to provide them with Gods or Goddesses? Well it would be a challenge to find enough information on such deities even if one wished to do so. The Bards corrupted their myths long before they fell silent. However they may be found in the Tir Andoman if one searches hard enough. It is not the policy of the Merlin to say what one seeks to worship, but one might ask why is it necessary for someone who tries to see Amhran in all things in Nature; does he or she look for a small part of it in a God or Goddess? If you must worship something worship the Mather who is represented by the Moon and the Ather who is represented by the Sun and look for Amhran in all things. However because in your later work you may meet some British, Gallic, Irish and Scottish Gods and Goddesses in the Tir Andoman and they may prove useful there is enclosed a list of some which are mentioned in the Order's records.

Andraste, protector Goddess of the Iceni
Anu, protector Goddess of Munster in Ireland
Badhbh, war Goddess and battle crow
Belenus, the Sun
Briganatia, protector Goddess of the Brigantes
Cernnunos, Antler headed God of the Hunt
Chrom Cruach (Irish) God of evil and discord
Conventina, Goddess of the Springs at
 Carrawburgh
Dagda, the Good Father

Epona, Horse Goddess of roads and pathways
Lugh, the Many skilled.
Macha, horse Goddess of roads and pathways
Maponos, Music and hunting
Morrigan, Victory, Prophecy, confusion and war.
Nemhain, war goddess, battle fury
Nodens, a healer
Ogma, a Warrior and Writer.
Oenghus, Love and Youth
Taranis, Thunder God

Important Festivals

Throughout the year the tempo of the Great Song changes. At the four points when that the tempo changes there is a lull where it is neither one nor the other. Thus the year is divided into eight - four neutral and four divisions. These are from November the 1st to February the 1st, February the 1st to May 1st, May 1st to August 1st and August 1st to November 1st.

At the cusp of each, a festival was held. These had varying names between tribes but generally were called Samhain, Imbolc, Beltine, and Bron Trogain.

Samhain, in the beginning of November started the New Year. At a practical level, it was the time that most tribes had their annual gatherings to make laws, but this festival was a day of danger for upon these non-days Amhran was the weakest and discord was more likely to arise.

It was on these days that the veils between this world and the Tir Andoman is at its thinnest. The dead could also walk on those days including those of forgotten Gods and Goddesses. Such beings were invited to attend tribal gatherings so that their wisdom could contribute to the current knowledge of the Tribe. Often the Druids would bring bones of the ancestors to such meetings as symbols of the wisdom of the ancestors.

Beltine was also dangerous for then it was said that the Hollow Hills would open and the faery folk would walk, looking for suitable partners and babies. It is observable that faery activity on that day is far greater than the other lull days. In early days the villages would choose the most beautiful child or maiden from among themselves and offer them to the faery on that night in the hope that they might leave the rest of the village alone. This form of sacrifice was rarely taken as faeries do not often enter the dwellings of men as there is too much metal.

By performing rites with the public on those days it was hoped that we could protect them by making them ready to hear the new song in the next quarter. These were the public rites and were generally presided over by the Priest caste. Each Druid caste also had its own rites that were celebrated in private and were generally held to be deeper aspects of their own mysteries.

In addition, we celebrated the Equinox and Solstices (longest and shortest days) however again these were considered mysteries, which were not held with the public in attendance. The reason for this is because the date of these days changes, and for millennia this was considered an important secret. It was also because we were more interested in the worship of the Ather (Sun) who was worshiped at Equinoxes and Solstices the Mather (Moon at full and new Moon).

Thus, in addition to their normal rites, a Druid is expected to perform either personal or group workings on the days of the four seasons, the Equinox and Solstice, and minor rites on the days of the full and new moon. The rites of the new and full moon are personal rites.

Of the Druid Egg.

During thy initiation thou wast given a painted egg of stone[6]. About it in colours were painted an image of thine own Ubh or halo of fire which is about thee. This Ubh is a most excellent of representations and is a magical symbol of thine own powers and

---

[6] In the later years of the Order this egg was made of clear or rose crystal. It had three rings painted upon it and either a face or a sun (so called Celtic) Cross above it. It was held by a bronze or golden chain so that it hung above the heart. It was supposed to be kept in the secret compartment of a locked box which was supposed to be bequeathed to the Merlin of the Order upon the death of the Druid. Three months after the Druid's death the Merlin would ritually smash the egg to help free him from the Underworld.

strength. It must be cared for as it is a symbol of the Ather, the Mather and Amhran as being living presences in thy self. The three rings drawn upon it show the three worlds of the Amhran, the colours are those of thine own Ubh perceived with the second sight of the Merlin. Note well the colours placed upon the surface of the rock for these are the true colours of Amhran inside thee and the music that they shall play is your part of Amhran.[7]

It was born of the twin serpents after thy three-fold death and rebirth during the rite. It is a reminder that while the uninitiated have auras that are weak and full of impurity, thine own aura needs to be a Rock and pure.

This egg can be thy refuge in times of need. Hold it before thy mind's eye and in fantasy visualise thyself at its heart. Then if anyone would harm thee with a curse, or faery weapon, they will find their intended injury dashed upon the surface of the stone.

Of the Rite Stones or Timbers

Each Pendragon should acquire either twenty stones or twenty appropriate timbers that correspond to the Signs of the Zodiac and the Wanderers. They should be some measure of the Druid, either the span of the hand, the length of their cubit, or his height. Each should be marked with the rune of the Ogham and the seal of the sign of the zodiac and their personal seal.

The Ancient Druids tuned their magical stone circles unto the labour that each was to perform. Thus some were turned so that the Sun struck a certain stone at a particular time of day, while others were turned to reveal the Moon's cycles. Still others followed the procession of the Equinoxes and Solstices and others the Midsummer or Midwinter Sun. These are specialist works that are not the labour of the first degree. It is enough for thy temple to be built in accordance to the state Zodiac and the position of the Wanderers, therefore place thou the Lion stone in the East and the planets in their order in a anti-clockwise from that point.

In the centre place the Sun stone and about a pace in front of it Amhran Stone. At a pace from that place the Moon Stone and a

---

[7] Each colour has a musical note and Ogham attributed to it

The First grade - Measog

Arrangement of Temple Stones

pace from that place the Saturn Stone. Then in the East place the Jupiter stone and then the Mercury Stone a pace before it. In the south place the Venus Stone and the North, the Mars Stone. (See diagram) Thus you have created your sacred temple, if you have built it within your grove so much the better. If you perform your bi-weekly rites within such a circle, power will start to build up in the stones even if you are not present.

If a temporary temple has been built using the stones or timber, care must be taken in their storage. They should be placed in an Oak box upon which the M Ogham letter should be carved or painted on the inside bottom, top and on each side. This shall prevent any energy escaping.

Each Stone or timber should be communed with after its marking and wine or mead should be poured as a libation. This will enable the Druid to tune the stone to its particular note. It is an effective method to chant the correct note at the stones until they respond.

Rite of the Moon

Each Druid was supposed to perform a short rite to the moon twice a month, once on the new moon and again on the full moon. The opening and closing of these rites, which are essentially directed at the Mather in her different forms are incredibly ancient. Although the language was tidied up a bit in the 1880's there are references which will have the modern reader wondering. I would have written versions that removed such references or replaced them with clearer ones but somehow these lacked the power of the original. The simple beauty of it and the imagery that it spontaneously creates has lead me to some of my most mystical experiences. It is best performed outside although this is not often possible and within the stone or timber 'temple' described above. If there are times that you cannot get all this equipment it can be worked without it. Ideally it should be done under the light of the full or new moon, but again so long as it is done on the 'day'. As you can see, it is not so important that the rite is performed perfectly just that it is performed. The rite sets up a link between you and the Mather, which over time has a dramatic effect. Historians among you might be interested to know that the wine which is dabbed on the moon stone is a substitute for blood.

Mark out the space to be Purified with the dagger and say:-

No creature from the Tir Andoman may enter this circle without my blessing.

Turn to face the Moon stone and touch it. Look upward and say.

Silver Mather of Ner's dream
White sea flood of the Tir Andoman

> *Let thy caldron of creation inspire me*
> *Let thy Ubh become my crown*
> *Let thy note become my song.*

Sing the note

> *OOOOOOOOOOOOOOOO.*

Do this to the extent of thy breath thrice.

For when the Moon is at her fullness

Pour a little wine on the Moon stone and say:-

> *At thy time of fullness I offer this gift*
> *That I may hear the note of the Mather*
> *In the Moon of Plenty.*
> *For nothing is given without sacrifice.*

When thou hast finished commune with the moon to see what she shall tell thee. Then say:-

> *Mother of all I hear thee, I feel thee, I speak thy song for now and until the day where the Oinacos hears the completed Song and Knows.*

For when the Moon is at her newness

Pour a little wine on the Moon stone and say:-

> *At thy nativity I offer this sacrifice*
> *That I may hear Song of the Mather*
> *For nothing is given without sacrifice.*

When thou hast finished commune with the moon to see what she shall tell thee. Then say:-

> *Mother of all I hear thee, I feel thee, I speak thy song for now and until the day where the Oinacos hears the completed Song and Knows.*

On the rites of the Moon by a Druid.

After all these months performing these rites in what can only be described as dryness I can finally say that the Mather finally spoke to me in a way which is purely magical.

There was nothing unusual about the rite I did on Tuesday. It was the same hill, the same view of the rising moon over the sea, even the same brand of wine.

What was different was when I poured the wine upon the rock and part of me felt as if I was sacrificing my own blood. The wine seemed to absorb into the marble taking me with it.

I looked up and all around me was silver and still. I heard the OOOOO chant of the moon, but it was as if it were sung by a million voices. Then all I can say was that I was her, the Mather I mean.

I could feel the all of creation being created and destroyed within me. I felt waves of motion and yet felt totally calm. It is sad that there are no real words for the rest of it. I felt comforted and powerful at the same time.

Since this has happened I have been incredibly sensitive and able to understand others thoughts and feelings. I have also been aware of my own with a degree of clarity. It is as if I had just had a meeting with an incredibly wise woman who was able to see my soul and tell me what was wrong. Yet I felt it was all done with kindness and that my shortcomings are all part of Amhran too.

Initiation into the First Grade of Measog

Rulers of the Grove.

All Druids, including Rulers of the Grove should wear normal clothes and eggs and carry their staffs. Torches (or candles and lanterns).

Merlin: Pendragon bracelets, Staff of Oak. (The candidate's staff should be at hand as well as the prepared Druid's egg).
White Pendragon: White Pendragon staff, a spear, hammer.
Red Pendragon: Red Pendragon staff, a shield, with Caldron with potion[8], Wine (there should be a large cauldron of water

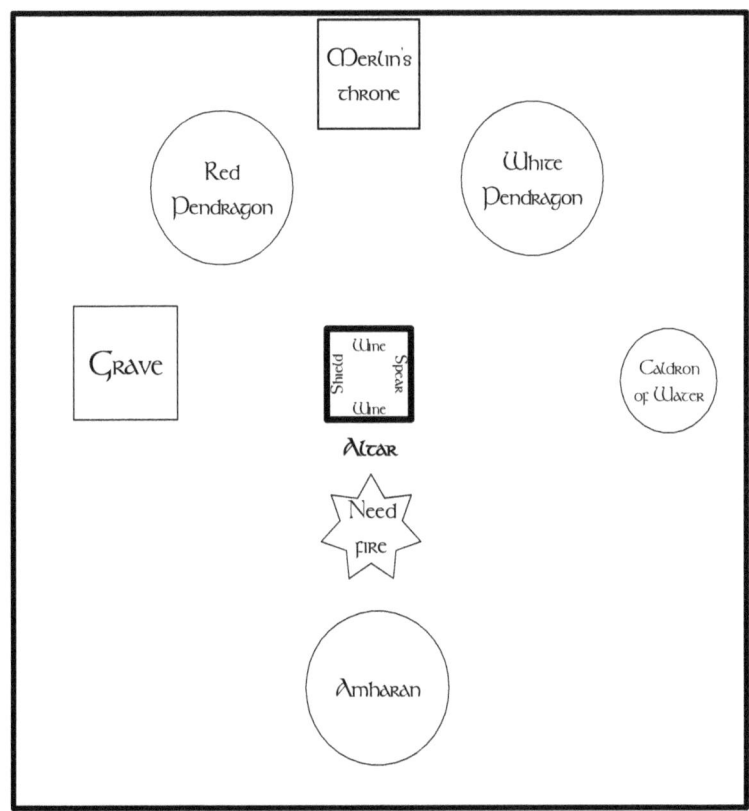

The Grove in the First Grade of Measog

---

[8] In my day the Potion was simply a few sprigs of holly, wheat and mead. However I am told that a few decades before a small amount of Laudanum

in the west), Garrotte about neck.

Amhran[9]: With seven stringed harp, mirror of Bronze.

The candidate should have fox fur tied around his right arm.[10] They should be given a cake made with Holly to eat while they wait and should be placed out of earshot of the rite. They should be given an egg with the Ogham of the first and last letters of their name painted on it.

On the altar should be the spear, the shield, wine in a bowl and corn. Before it a lit torch or a small fire. To the right of that a cauldron of water. In the north should be dug a square hole about two feet deep long enough to lay the candidate crouched. If a natural stream is unavailable place a trough of water in the East.

The Setting Aside

Amhran walks to the Merlin who hands him a dagger of Iron. Amhran then walks behind him and in a clockwise circle that encloses the whole rite (excluding the candidate) thrice. As this is done he says:-

> *I set aside this place in Bith*
> *I set aside this place in the Tir Andoman*
> *I set aside this place in the Mag Mor*
> *In this Kingdom Time is Not*
> *In this Kingdom Light and Darkness are Not*
> *In this Kingdom All things are Oinacos*
> *I seal this place with the Ring-Pass-Not of Iron*
> *I seal this place in the Name of the Mather*

---

was added as this was more convenient than the 'milk of the poppy' which was described in the early rites.

[9] Amhran should be the opposite sex to the candidate.

[10] The candidate should be also warned beforehand that what he or she is about to do will be frightening and unpleasant at points. They should be assured that no actual physical harm will be done to them despite the drama involved. There is nothing worse than a candidate running off. I have been told that it has not happened, but it is better to be safe than sorry.

I seal this place in the Name of the Ather.
I seal this place in the Name of the Song which binds.

Amhran gives the Knife of Iron to the Merlin and goes before the Altar.

He plays a scale on the Harp.

Merlin: (striking staff): *The riddle is born. I am one and alone, yet I Create Three. Who am I?*

White Pendragon: *Light*

Red Pendragon: *Dark*

Amhran: *Thou art the circle of fire. Thou art the Night's dark sky pricked with the Light of the Stars.*

Merlin: *How did I create?*

White Pendragon: *With the White Pendragon of Fire.*

Red Pendragon: *With the Red Pendragon of Water.*

Amhran: *Taking both Pendragons entwined in thy arms you created the first Breath and the first Stone.*

Merlin raises arms in the Position of Creation and then crashes bracelets together and then sings:

OOOOOOOOOOOOOOOOOOOOOOOOOOOOOOO
UUUUUUUUUUUUUUUUUUUUUUUUUUUUUUU
EEEEEEEEEEEEEEEEEEEEEEEEEEEEEEE

As he sings OOOOOOOO so does the White Pendragon sing OOOOOOOO. When he sings UUUUUUUUUU likewise does the Red Pendragon sings UUUUUUUUUUUUUUUUU and when EEEEEEEEEEEEE Amhran sings EEEEEEEEEEEEEE.

Merlin: *Why did I create?*

White Pendragon: *For it is thine own self.*

Red Pendragon: *To Name thyself.*

Amhran: *To hold a perfect image of thyself to know who thou art.*

Merlin: *Show me my image.*

Amhran plays seven notes and then light the torches or lanterns on each of the stones. Then when he is finished the holds up his mirror and says:-

Amhran: *Behold the Song and the Singer.*

All take their staffs and knock three times three on the ground. The Amhran plays the scale of seven notes.

The Rite of the Three-Fold Sacrifice

Merlin: *Caste of the Druid Order of Pendragon Hear the words of the Merlin. A fox touches our boundaries seeking to be reborn a Druid. His cunning hath brought him thus far and now he seeketh to see the Universe.*

Amhran: *The Amhran is in his breast and he knows his path will lead him to death and sacrifice.*

Merlin: *Then bring him forth and let him die so that in his three-fold-death he shall be reborn in all things.*

Amhran returns with the candidate and they enter in the West.

Merlin: *Fox where cometh thou from?*

The Candidate (Prompted by Amhran): *From the Lands of the South to the Lands of the West where the sun now sets.*

Merlin: *Why cometh thou fox? Thy place is in the South where thou ruleth among the lands of Bith.*

The Candidate (Prompted by Amhran): *I request a boon. I wish to hear the Song Amhran and be reborn as a Druid.*

Merlin: *Such a boon will mean that you will sacrifice thy earthly life thrice. Once for Amhran, Once for the*

Mather and Once for the Ather only then shall a Fox be a Druid.

The Candidate: *I am willing to offer this and other Earthly lives in the quest to be a Druid.*

Merlin: *Thy offer is accepted. For nothing is achieved without sacrifice.*

Amhran: *What have you there for me?*

The Candidate hands him the Egg and the wheat.

Amhran: *The Fox offers me the Egg of his life and his seed.*

Merlin: *Venerate the sacrifice.*

The Red Pendragon comes forth. Takes the bowl of the potion from the altar and gives it to the candidate to drink. Then she takes him to the cauldron where he kneels before it and places the noose around his neck.

Red Pendragon: *I am the Mather of All. In my belly you were given life and I have the power to take it away again so that you may be reborn. Doest thou agree?*

When the candidate nods she thrusts his head under the water and draws it out with the noose tight around his neck and says:-

Death hath come by the noose, Fox thou art no more.

The White Pendragon comes forth with a hammer.

White Pendragon: *I am the Ather of All. The fires within you are my fires, wilst thou extinguish them so that you may be reborn?*

When the candidate nods he strikes him with the hammer and says:-

Death hath come with lightening, Fox thou art no more.

Amhran extinguishes the torch (or the fire with water from the Cauldron). The White and Red Pendragon take the Candidate through the water to the East.

Merlin: *Thou has died twice Fox would thou do so again to be reborn as a Druid?*

When Candidate nods Merlin says:

> *Thrice thou hast requested this boon, now thrice you shall die.*

The candidate is turned to face Amhran who crushes the egg in front of his face. He is then turned to face the Merlin who draws the knife across his neck. The Red Pendragon pours red wine over his head.

Merlin: *Death hath come with a swift knife, Fox thou art no more.*

Amhran, and the two Pendragons take the candidate to the grave and lay in him a crouched position facing the West. They take the spear, the Shield etc and lay them over the top of him then place the bowl of Wine at his feet and then sprinkle the corn over him. They cover the grave with a cloak.

Amhran: *The Fox is dead and the land is better for his Blood. Yet his spirit still requests to be made a Druid.*

Merlin: *Is he thrice born?*

Amhran: *He had died the three fold sacrifice.*

Merlin: *Then let him enter Tir Andoman.*

The Pendragons beat their sticks on either side of the grave nine times. Then they retreat to stand before the brook or water trough. The cloak is removed and Amhran says:-

> *Tarry not in thy Grave, if Thou would be a Druid thou must Journey through the Tir Andoman to the land of the Ather.*

The candidate rises from the grave and Amhran removes the fox fur and casts it in the grave.

Amhran: *Thou hast been a fox, thou art no longer*
Thou has been a farmer, thou art no longer

Thou has been a Mather thou art no longer
Thou has been warrior, thou art no longer
What thou art to become lies in the Tir Andoman
In that land look neither left nor right,
Neither up nor down.
Take no food nor water.
Talk to none but she who would answer thy purpose.

The candidate is led betwixt the Pendragons and into the water trough. Then to the altar. The Red Pendragon takes the candidate's staff from the Merlin and goes to the east of altar.

Red Pendragon: *Thrice dead Man (or Woman) if thou wishes to be a Druid you must make a terrible Oath and place thyself under great and terrible Geissie. Art thou willing?*

When the candidate nods. She adds: -

Then take in your left hand this staff and place it upon the ground. Then stretch your right arm to the sky and raise your right leg[11]. Then repeat after me:

The Oath

I who am half man and half tree
I who have my feet on the ground and can touch the sky
I who am a creature of flaming water
I who am in a place that is no-where and everywhere
Do bind myself unto the Druidic Order of Pendragon
For this life and unto others
I freely and willingly accept the following Geissie on my life
I shall not speak the earthly name any member of the Order.
I shall not reveal any of its teachings or rites.

---

[11] In your left hand is the staff which is rooted in the ground. Then stretch your right arm to the sky and raise your right leg. It might seem a bizzare position, but is similar to a position one used by a Druid in dark age texts. This is called the Gesture of Power

I shall not seek power for its own sake
I shall not claim a financial reward for the Work of the Order
I shall not spread discord.
I shall look for Amhran in all things
And seek to find the Oinacos in all.
I swear this
By the Sun, the Moon
The Wanderers.
By the Earth, by the plants,
By the animals.
By Men
By the Gods
May I be shunned by all creation if I break this oath
And may the sky fall on me
And the earth swallow me up
May I wander lost in the Tir Andoman and never find the Isle of the Blessed.

Red Pendragon: *Now place thy hands on thy head and say 'I give my head unto the Order'*

Candidate does so. Red Pendragon and the White Pendragon stand four paces from the Merlin and place their staves in an arch.

Merlin: *Thy time in the Underworld is complete. Now venture forth into the lands of the Blessed*

Amhran escorts the Candidate underneath the arch but stands back so that he forms a triangle with the Red and White Pendragons. The Merlin stands.

Merlin: *Who art tho who enters the Land of the Blessed?*

Amhran: *One who was a fox.*
  One who was a farmer
  One who was a Wife
  One who was a Warrior
  One who would be a Druid.

Merlin: *To be a Druid one must have an Ubh of Stone built by the power of the Pendragons and the seed of the Oinacos. Yet you have no Ubh of Stone and the seed of the Oinacos sleeps as in deepest winter*

Amhran: *The Ubh of the Fox was crushed in the Three Fold Death. It was not worthy of a Druid.*

Merlin: *An Ubh that was lost in the three fold sacrifice shall be returned unto thee three fold strong. For Nothing is Achieved without Sacrifice. Let it be so.*

The Pendragons walk three times around the candidate while Amhran plays the seven note scale on harp. All Sing the Seven Notes of the Wanderers with the Letter of Amhran.

Merlin: *About you shineth the Ubh of Stone of a Druid. It is a body that will endure forever. Now it is time to awaken the seed so that you shall be a worthy chariot for the Rider of Forever.*

He places the Druid's Ubh over the candidate's head and then bids him to stand in the Gesture of Power. He holds the Ubh over the candidate's breast and says:-

Merlin: *Thou who art half man and half tree, thou who walks betwixt worlds whose feet touch the earth, whose hands reach heaven. Thou who is a creature of flaming water. Within thy breast is the seed of the Oinacos. Let it awaken as we call its holy name.*

[White Pendragon sings the AAAAAAAAAAAAAAAA. Red Pendragon sings the OOOOOOOOOOOOOOOOO. Amhran Sings the UUUUUUUUUUUUUUUUU. This is done simultaneously. The Merlin sees an acorn of brilliance in the candidates breast start to awaken and sends forth a shoot.]

When this happens the Merlin seals the Ubh and the seed in the candidate by drawing the sign of the Sun upon his forehead, throat and breast with wine.

Merlin: *You shall be known among us as* [the name of the Tree which is the wood of the candidate's staff] *of* [address][12] . *Go forth into Nature as a Measog*

The new Measog is escorted from the temple by Amhran until after the Rite is completed.

The Closure

Merlin (striking staff and stands in the position of Power): *I am half man and half tree, who walks betwixt worlds whose feet touch the earth and whose hands reach heaven. Within my breast is the seed of the Oinacos. In its name I make the three worlds one again.*

[White Pendragon sings the AAAAAAAAAAAAAAAA. Red Pendragon sings the OOOOOOOOOOOOOOOOO. Amhran Sings the UUUUUUUUUUUUUUU. This is done simultaneously].

Merlin: *The riddle is answered the rite is done the worlds are aligned. Let us depart unto our groves in peace.*

Address to the New Measog

No doubt you would be aware that the rite you have just performed was not simply a piece of theatre in which you were a participant. Instead it was a journey where you were seeing the magical forces that were operating upon you at that moment. Much of the rite will yield much to contemplation and you must feel that you can approach the Merlin if there is anything that you fail to understand or any information that you discover in your revere.

Many books may be written on this rite, however a basic outline may be described to you now.

It is based on the Mystery of the Myth of Creation, which you have been handed to memorise. You are playing the role of Amhran as it is sacrificed to give life to the world. But the rite turns the

---
[12]The place names attempted to be as close as possible to the person's real town, village or suburb or while remaining poetic. For example Hazel of Sherwood would be good as would Rowan of Marlow [Street], Ash of Railway [Street} would not be, neither would Willow of High [Road]. The Merlin had considerable leeway in naming people once calling someone 'the Brook' when 'the Canal' might have been more appropriate.

myth on its head as it shows a path to return through the Three Worlds to the Oinacos.

Firstly you entered the circle wearing a fox fir on your right arm, you were also called after the fox. Now in ancient society the fox was seen as the most clever of animals and in his most primitive state so was man. Thus by identifying with the fox you are saying that you are a man in his most primitive state, cunning but limited. Your right arm is the hand that you will reach to heaven in when standing in the gesture of power and therefore wearing it indicates that all you can draw upon is your animal self.

To become something more than a simple animal you are told that you must die and be reborn thrice. You agree and hand Amhran an Ubh, which has your name written upon it in Ogham which represents your normal frail mortal self. It is worth mentioning that up until a hundred years ago the Ubh would have your blood on it as a symbol of your self.

After the simple decision to die to your mundane life, you are given a drink that contains holly and mead which is an offering traditionally made to those who have agreed to give their lives as a sacrifice.

Then begins the three-fold death. The Druid who represents the Mather places your head underwater. This act places you into the Tir Andoman, which is often represented as a Kingdom that can be entered through pools of water. However your body is on dry land that means you are paradox in two worlds at once - indeed a walker between worlds. You are drawn by the noose out of the water symbolising your death in this world as a result of what you have seen in the Tir Andoman.

This symbolises the part of the myth where the Mather cooks Amhran in a cauldron but his spirit is still alive.

Next you were taken to the Ather who hits you with his hammer that symbolises lightning. This act should have weakened your Ubh so that it can be easily broken in the next stage of the rite.

During the next phase you have your throat cut in a symbolic manner, i.e. without hazard. No doubt you were aware that the red wine symbolises blood in this rite. Wine is a good symbol for blood because it is created by the sacrifice of the life of yeast and sugar to create alcohol - which is something new. In the olden times the blood of a fox or chicken replaced this.

You are then placed in your grave in the manner of pre-historic times. The spear represents your power, the shield represents your body, the seed is your knowledge and the wine is your blood. Together they represent the four elements' Spear (Fire), Shield (Earth), Wine (Water), Seed (Air).

You are awoken from the sleep of death by nine knocks - one for each of the three worlds, three times, and taken to the Tir Andoman. This is symbolised by you stepping across water. You are advised how to avoid the terrors of the Tir Andoman and to only speak to the Mather, lest you become trapped there.

You are also told that you are no longer a fox but have died and been reborn a farmer, a wife and a warrior. These are the positions of ordinary people in the Celtic world. Notice that there are no craftspeople or priests mentioned. This is because those professions were considered 'magical' and is part of the new life that you are seeking.

The Mather extracts a terrible oath from you. She uses a word called geissie, which is a Celtic word meaning life condition in which you agree. Later Medieval myths describe Celtic heroes having all sorts of geissie ranging from not eating certain foods to not wearing certain colours. Failure to obey such geissie always results in the death of the hero in tragic circumstances.

You make an oath in what we call the Position of Power. This has you leaning on your staff with your left leg raised and your right hand extended to heaven. In this strange position you declare yourself half man, half tree, touching the heavens and with your foot on earth. This is a statement that you are a true reflection of the Oinacos in its creation. You reflect the four elements your feet is on the earth, your hand in the air, you are described also as a creature of flaming water. You also reflect all of creation being animal, rock, sky creature and plant. It is worth pointing out that this position was described in ancient texts as being the stance taken by Druids when they were conjuring.

During the Oath you give your head to the Order. The Celts placed a considerable emphasis on the head which they saw as the seat of all power. It was believed that if you cut the head off a person you placed them in your power in the Tir Andoman. They decorated their temples with the heads of sacrifices to indicate that the three fold death which the sacrifice had made was channelling its power into the temple.

After the oath you are then taken to the realm of the Ather or the land of the Blessed. You are then given a new Ubh to replace the one, which was shattered during the three-fold death. This 'stone egg', an emblem of which you are given to wear over your heart, a lot stronger than the Ubh of an ordinary man and is designed to repel the sort of magical attacks of faery folk and others who might do you harm. It is created by the positive and negative actions of the Pendragon's staves more of which you will be taught in later degrees. The staves energies are tuned and further 'flavoured' by the notes of Amhran's harp, which play the notes of the seven Wanderers. In astrology these seven planets affect a man's character and the act of playing the note impresses the Ubh with what the planets should be, rather than what they may have been during the nativity. This creates the ideal Ubh for a Druid to reside within and work magic later.

The last phase is the most profound for it awakens the Divinity within the person. It enables them to truly be a Druid. The Oinacos is awakened by calling its name, which is so powerful three people in harmony vibrate different parts of it.

You are told to go forth into Nature as a Measog. You are not permitted to see the closing of the rite at this point, just as you were not permitted to see the opening. This indicates that your real journey as a Druid is solitary and is not found within the Order, which only opens the gateways for you to find Amhran and then the Oinacos in all.

Of the Rulers of the Grove

General

The Rulers of the Grove in the first-degree rite represent the forces at play in the great myth of creation. The Merlin is the Oinacos, the Red Pendragon is the Mather and the White Pendragon is the Ather and Amhran is in part represented by the officer with that name and in part by the Candidate. With the obvious exception of the Candidate all must seek to move themselves into a state of communion with the faces of the Oinacos they represent. To each Druid appointed a role in this rite is assigned the task of entering into a communion with these aspects of the One so that this force brims over into the rite. For this reason they are tasks that can only be allocated to the most experienced of Druids. Experience is only attained by contemplation of the matters of the higher degree.

Merlin

Wears two bracelets with the Red Pendragon on his Right Arm and the White Pendragon on his left. The serpents should coil about the forearms thrice and have their heads pointing to the centre of the wrist. His arms should never be pointed at the ground while he wears these bracelets. On his brow in red paint or wine should be the solar cross, which haveth a direct correspondence with the action of the Oinacos in Earth. He has a staff of Hazel and an iron knife in his belt upon which is written in Ogham AOU in a triangle.

Red Pendragon

Has a six foot staff of Apple with a Pendragon looped around it thrice and then extended. The Pendragon shall be forged of copper. The red Pendragon should also have bracelets of iron, a noose about her neck and a small cauldron hanging from a belt of calf leather. On her brow in red paint or wine should be drawn the sign of the crescent cup. Note that the wands of the Pendragon should never be pointed at the ground for this would create discord.

White Pendragon

Has a six foot staff of Hazel with a Pendragon looped around it thrice and then extended. The Pendragon shall be forged of iron. The white Pendragon should also have bracelets of copper and a hammer in a belt of calf leather. On his brow in red paint or wine should be drawn the sign of the upright sword. Note that the wands of the Pendragon should never be pointed at the ground for this would create discord.

Amhran

Has a seven stringed harp and a mirror of bronze to reflect all to the Oinacos in a belt of calf leather. On his brow in red paint or wine should be drawn the letter U in Ogham.

Of the Blessing of the fluids and fires

Before each rite the fluids, fires and implements shall be blessed in an appropriate manner. The Wine should be blessed by Amhran, the Water by the Mather, the Fires by the Ather and the other implements by the Merlin.

Of the Wine

The Ruler of the Rite pertaining to Amhran should take the wine betwixt his hands and say:-

> *This is my blood which was poured out upon the world to give it life for Nothing is achieved without sacrifice. By this song I bring it closer unto my perfected note.*

He sings his note (UUUUUUUUUUUUUUUUUUUU) until the wine starts to glow with the power of the note. He then sayeth:-

> *Thus has the blood become my sacrifice by association.*

Of the Water

The Ruler of the Rite pertaining to the Red Pendragon should take each item of water. Stand in the position of power while looking upon the water.

> *This is the Water of the Mather born in the Cauldron of the Tir Andoman. By this song I bring it to my perfected note.*

She sings her note (OOOOOOOOOOOOOOOOOOO) until the water starts to glow with light. She then sayeth:-

> *Thus hath the water become the Mather by association.*

Of the Fires

The Ruler of the Rite pertaining to the White Pendragon should light each candle, torch or fire. Then standing in the position of power looking upon the flame should say:-

> *This spark is part of the Flame of creation which encircles and abides throughout all creation. By this song I bring it to my perfected note.*

He sings his note (AAAAAAAAAAAAAAAAAAAA) until the fire glows with a different light.

> *Thus hath the fire become the Ather by association.*

Of the wands and other implements

All these shall be placed within a pace of the Merlin who shall stand in the position of power and say:-

> *All things were born in the mind of the Oinacos, Mather, Ather, Amhran are all containers of my light that is No Light. I draw down the power of the Oinacos to dwell among these tokens that it may empower them and learn from them.*

The Merlin stands in this pose while light cometh down from the heavens and indwells in each item.

Chapter Three

The Second Grade – Ovate

While the work of the First Degree is about the Amhran and providing life to the Material World, the Second Degree is attributed to the Mother, Tir Andoman, the Ancestors and Death. Ideally rites and meditations should be done in a cave or barrows, although some barrows did have the original inhabitants who more than once caused some problems for several of our members! Fortunately in the area where I lived there was a delightful little cave where I was unlikely to be disturbed. Others used to do their work in cellars or among their coal.

This is also the Grade where the Druids work with Gods and Goddesses. This is because much of the work involves journeys to the Tir Andoman which is populated by the dead and Gods and Goddesses which have been forgotten on Earth and cannot be drawn to influence the minds and hearts of people any longer. Such Gods are sometimes melancholy creatures and other times can be the source of great wisdom. They are not simply Celtic, I have met several semi-deified humans and a couple of forgotten saints that are similar to Gods and Goddesses. I also have found it interesting that some of the more obscure British Christian sects whose worship is long forgotten have their 'heavens' in Tire Andoman. In theory Tir Andoman should link the Gods and Goddesses of all nations, not just those of the West. But however hard I have tried I have been unable to find them. Perhaps a

Westerner like myself can only access that part of Tir Andoman that is linked to his culture. All creatures in the Tir Andoman are either men or created by men and as such all partake of the Discord to some degree or another.

Of Tir Andoman

Tir Andoman is the realm of the Mather and is like an infinite cauldron containing energy much like water. Within this water all the memories of the Amhran are kept and all the Gods, Goddesses, the dead, and Elves dwell.

Once it was believed that this world existed below the earth or on the other side of lakes (particularly those clear enough to mirror the scenery around their rim). This is only partly true as the Tir Andoman exists at right angles to this one overlapping it entirely[1] just as Mag Mor is at right angles to it. While caves, and lake edges are methods of entering the Tir Andoman it is more because they are potent tokens of what the Tir Andoman is like.

Tir Andoman is divided into three. There is the land of the Dead (Tir Naharbh), The Land of the Gods and the Lands of Faery (Tir Nashidhe). There is also a half-world that borders upon it that is shaped by the mind of the individual experiencing it. Thus in the initial stages of a journey to that land, Tir Andoman looks much like the world of Bith that you have just departed, indeed it is almost a mirror image.

As a person gets further away from the entrance to Bith, the Tir Andoman starts to get more chaotic, much like a dream where one strange image slides into another. These images are all created by the mind of the observer and have only a meaning for him or her. It is during this phase that much discord is created because beings seem to appear and offer the inexperienced Druid much. They will seek to flatter him with promises of power or important teaching. Knowing the differences between thine own discord and real Tir Andoman entities is one of the most difficult lessons of the Second Degree.

---

[1] The more modern way of saying this is that 'it is in another dimension'.

This part of Tir Andoman is where you visit when you are asleep. It is rare that one would, in Sleep experience the deeper realms of Tir Andoman. However we journey unto this realm to recharge our Ubh of Fire from the Emerald Heart of the Earth. If we fail to visit this place, even for a night, our Ubh will lose its vitality and its ability to keep the body alive diminishes. One must spend at least four hours in Tir Andoman in sleep to keep one's Ubh functioning. It is preferable that one spends six in that place to receive the full blessing of the Amhran.

As you move deeper into the Tir Andoman these images and beings will move away and be replaced by more random and less controllable images. You will start to experience those beings that you wished to truly contact. These will be Gods and Goddesses, if these are what you wish to see, or ancestors or Faery.

If at this point you wish to meet a particular person the scene will change and you will be carried rapidly to that person's portion of the Tir Andoman. The scenery will be their idea of what they deserve in the Tir Andoman for good or for discord. For in the Tir Andoman it is possible for a soul to create for himself a deep hell, if that is what he thinks he deserves.

Often family and friends, some who are dead and others who are simply visiting in their dreams will surround them. They may or may not be seeing you depending how much in tune you are to their note. For this reason it is easier to contact dead ancestors in your own family line than it is to contact those to whom you have a looser connection. Former Merlins are an exception as they are tuned to your note by virtue of your first degree initiation and if your initiator is dead you will have a stronger bond with him than anyone else other than your nearest kin.

The dead may travel back to earth once a year during the festival known as Samhain; it is then that they visit their kin and it was a custom to leave food out for them. Generally they lack any power to do more than watch their families grow, but sometimes those with the Sight see them. They are swept back to the Tir Andoman when the veil starts to harden making it difficult to stay.

The Tir Andoman also contains those creatures created by the will of man and the Amhran - the Gods and Goddesses. As we have said often these are not any divine beings as such, although they have tremendous powers. When a man creates a God he takes part of his own Amhran and builds a new form around it. Over time he places all of the powers that he himself has into this form and through his dedication that God sings. One man's God is small but if he managed to convince another of its power the form grows and can use the combined power of two to effect change in the world. Obviously these Gods have incredible power when a whole tribe worships them and can perform many miracles. But these powers are only the power of a single person magnified. It is said that every human has the power of a god but they know it not.

The God or Goddess dwells naturally in the Tir Andoman and it is the worship and dedication of the people who can draw it out and empower it. However like mankind who made them, the Gods and Goddesses are creatures of discord too - some, particularly those built on the concept of fear are entirely of discord. When the worship of any God or Goddess, good or bad is broken then, becoming aware that it will never be able to leave the Tir Andoman again, it arranges discords like war, plague or famine to remind its worshipers that it is still there. If it fails to attract the attention of its worshippers then it retreats into the Tir Andoman never to emerge again.

Gods and Goddesses combine the powers and knowledge of all the people who have ever worshipped them and can be extremely wise. They will always offer a visitor to the Tir Andoman great powers and favours if they start again their worship, for worship is the Gods or Goddesses' reason for being. There have been some who have attempted to do just this, but find that such a religion is born out of time. The Amhran does not repeat itself in exactly the same way twice and unless the religion is sufficiently adapted to modern times it will not survive. Some of the Gods and Goddesses will bend to meet the needs of the time, but there are others who will wear the clothing of the century only to eventually draw back its worshippers to an age no longer appropriate.

The Gods and Goddesses dwell deep within the Tir Andoman, the deeper you journey, the further back in the memory of the Amhran you will go. Each God and Goddess has a realm beholding unto his or her nature. Thou willst find smith gods in their forges, ruling gods in palaces, corn gods in fields, and war goddesses on the battlefield. There are sometimes the shells of their closest worshippers who believe themselves to be in a heaven. Of course their spirit is wiser and has moved on as the Oinacos will never remain worshipping such a small part of itself for long.

Deeper still in the Tir Andoman are the faery kingdoms of Tir Nashidhe although the faery folk can be found anywhere in this world and the Tir Andoman.

Tir Nashidhe is divided into one half, which is ruled by a King dwelleth the menfolk and the other, which is ruled by a Queen, is where the women faery dwell. Each faery kingdom has 12 lesser administrators who are a Prince or a Princess wherever appropriate. They oversee districts within Tir Nashidhe and the 12 faery guilds. These are the warriors, the priests, the builders, the jewellers, the potters, the fishermen, the horse handlers, the farmers, the shepherds, the cooks, the doctors and the musicians.

The Faery are dangerous and will often trick a person into staying with them. Eating is a trick that will anchor you into their domain and make you more real to them so that they can do thee more harm.

However you must not tarry with them, and instead demand to see the King and Queen who are the closest to humanity among this race. This is because in a time long ago these beings were worshipped and were given powers of the Amhran of men. As such they are more amenable to discourse with humans, although it would be perilous for humanity if they were to be worshipped again.

The last time men worshipped them ended in war between ended because of the widespread introduction of metal among humans. The name of the King and Queen were purposely forgotten by the people and the Druids and were never to be mentioned aloud, lest they take the opportunity to return.

Several thousand years of peace and a feeling of resignation that for now Bith belongs to the humans, means that the King and Queen are friendlier to humans who have not harmed their kind. Also, if requested directly, the Elves are obliged to take you to the King and Queen.

Unlike the Gods and Goddesses, Elves are able to leave the Tir Andoman. This is because they have an Ubh of Fire like humans and they can gain energy by eating in either Tir Andoman or Bith. This means that they feel as tired as we do during any journeys between this world and the next. They tend to make their journeys as the Amhran pauses at the end and beginning of the seasons when it is easier.

The King and Queen rarely leave Tir Andoman because it would cause them a dramatic loss in their powers. In the Underworld they have the combined power of all the humans and elves that worshipped them and mastery of the Emerald Heart of the Earth however in Bith they have only their own.

It is said that the King and Queen live separately because of a long standing feud however there are more magical reasons for this. Faeries mate but once a year on May Day. They often do this in earth because it is easier for them to conceive. But the King and Queen mate in Tir Nashidhe because the act enables them to bring together two tremendous magical forces that create fertility in their kingdom.

Until recently, it was believed that the mating of Kings and Queens in Bith also performed a similar function and it was considered bad for a Kingdom if a royal marriage was not blessed with children, as these represented the fertility of the land.

Now many of you have asked why the initiation ceremony makes no mention of the beings of Faery. This is because the rites of this Order give you power over beings in Tir Andoman. Alas, as humans, we have no rights over the Faery, indeed it is considered that one day they will replace humans on Bith when our time in the Song is over. In those days, the Spark will choose to live among them and we will merge into them. They, being immortal, will provide the Spark with a new perspective of itself, as we are limited in that regard.

On the Ancestors

The dead are with us always. After the Oinacos and Amhran has departed from their bodies what remains dwells in the Tir Andoman until the Song is complete. There it is kept alive by the Emerald

Heart of the Earth. The life that the Ubh of Fire has in the Tir Andoman is in measure to what it deserves, for that Kingdom is extremely fluid and a human mind that entereth creates what it wilt. But just as people will create palaces and Kingdoms of great beauty and adventure, so they shall populate it with demons and other creatures of fear. Thus when we journey into the Tir Andoman in search of our ancestors we will find them in beautiful kingdoms or hellish places depending on the character of the persons when they died.

In the Tir Andoman there is no opportunity for the dead to develop, for it is as if we are visiting the memory of the Amhran which remembers many different notes but no longer plays that particular line of music. When looking at such beings we should not think of them as people but rather as the empty carriage from which the driver has departed - they are a shadow of a being that is elsewhere in creation.

They have tremendous import for the Druid who wishes to find the knowledge and wisdom such beings may have had. Truly it is a library of information that may be tapped if you can find the right person to ask. Asking the right question of the right person and being able to hear the answer is one of the most important lessons of this grade.

The simile of the Library is apposite for Tir Andoman and the people you meet there are but books of knowledge, frozen in the time that they were published. Although it might be possible to contact one's dead mother in Tir Andoman it is futile to ask her about missing Druid lore if she had not been privy to that information while she was alive. Upon encountering Ptolemy, thou wilt be able to learn much about his system of astronomy but he will not be about to tell thee about Hershel[2]. Likewise the dead are unable to predict the future of life on Earth because most of them cannot depart the Tir Andoman to see it.

Sometimes there is a pathology where a being manages to leave the Tir Andoman or never arrives. Sometimes, when death is violent, or the attachment to earth is great, the person refuses to let go of their body. They insist that they are simply dreaming and refuse to stray far. The body may be interred and still the spirit will remain.

---

[2] Hershell is the old name for Uranus.

Now, since a man remaineth where his heart is, he will be drawn to places and people where he used to frequent. There those with the Sight who will see him and their recognition will lead him unto the false conclusion that he is still among the living. The dead person will be seen to appear and disappear at regular festivals or gatherings.

Such cases are generally harmless and will end when the spirit finally concedes that they are dead and should pass on to the Tir Andoman. If they fail to do so then the Amhran inside them will draw them to Tir Andoman after a short period of time and, being that he hath no body to provide him sustenance, he will not have the energy in the Shell of Fire to resist. They can prolong their stay by drawing energy from those living, particularly those who have blood ties. This is sometimes felt as a sudden chill as the Shell of Fire loses some of its heat. The sick, the young and especially babies might not have enough energy to sustain their Shells of Fire and might die as a result. For this reason the sick or the young should not be allowed too close to a dead person or a house where someone is recently deceased.

The dead may draw some energy from food that is specifically left out for them as offerings. These should be of things that swiftly decompose such as milk or meat that liberates energy in the process. Flowers, incense and blood are also extremely effective.

Such Taibhse (ghosts) still need their corpse to anchor them unto to the physical world and although they may not need to visit it, or even be aware of it, they remain attached to it through a line of magnetism that connects the area of the corpse to where the heart should be. This line goes upward through the top of the forehead where it is connected by a longer web line to the rest of the Ubh of Fire. Decapitating the corpse severs this line; the Ubh of Fire loses its anchor and swiftly moves to the Tir Andoman. In such cases, the head would have to be placed either some distance away from the neck or between the legs, to prevent one who knoweth the ways of death from attempting to reforge a connection.

In other cases, the Amhran might feel that an important message needeth to be delivered from the dead person to one living and will allow the Taibhse to be seen by the person and then depart.

There is another post-mortem event, little used in these times is where a person after death agrees to continue working in a task assigned for them by the Amhran. These were guardians of a Tribe. They were usually tied to a particular area where they would act as a walker between the worlds for the Tribe. Part of their body would be placed in the barrow or holy place that would act as a telegraph operator to call the person to the presence of the officiating Druid.

Their task was like a diplomat between Bith and the Tir Andoman, or, in some cases, the Mag Mor. They would make contacts with such beings who may be of assistance to the Tribe and ask them to step out of the Tir Andoman to assist. If they could assist but needed help in leaving the Tir Andoman then the 'diplomat' would approach the Tribe and tell them to make the appropriate sacrifices. This was particularly true of some Gods and Goddesses who had been forgotten over time but were suddenly 'rediscovered' (sometimes under new names) and worshipped again.

At various times in the history of Druidism it has been considered that too much reliance was placed upon some of these 'ambassadors' and not enough on common sense. There has always been a feeling that some of the older ones were unable to understand the needs of the people and they had become too powerful. The practice also degenerated to the point where the Druid was simply fortune telling for the tribe or approaching these 'ambassadors' with trivialities. At the same time it was noted that a force for discord was brewing in the Tir Andoman, attacks by the Faery Folk increased, a few of the Older Gods were worshipped when they should not have been and started causing plagues and some of the information that was coming through the Ambassadors was encouraging war rather than peace. It was decided to shut the barrows and many were closed. The process eventually weakened the 'ambassadors' in their tomb and over time most of them entered the Tir Andoman and did not return. In some areas the practice was continued by village priests with varying degrees of success but gradually broke down as Druids did not use it. In places where it continued, it was more as a result of superstition than anything else. But such barrows were not closed down and their 'ambassadors' remain to this day[3].

After a time the barrows were forgotten and the Druids developed other entry points to the Tir Andoman through caves and journeys into the Hollow Hills.

Now within Tir Andoman are beings called the Cucullati. These are three guardian spirits who have been appointed to guide and protect the Druid in the Other World. They appear as cloaked dwarfs whose faces cannot be seen. Two of them carry swords and one of them acts as the speaker for all three. You should call them upon your arrival into Tir Andoman and if they fail to appear then it is a sign that it is not thy time to enter that land.

When journeying through the lands of the ancestors thou should remember balance in all thy dealings. They are like you, but are not and one day part of you will be like they are now. Some will not see thee or wish to talk to thee, in that judgement they should be respected as someone who ignores thee in thy mundane world is respected. If someone asks you to leave them, this too should be respected. The world that they have created around them in Tir Andoman is their home to which they are incredibly attached.

Let not pity move thee if thou see an Ancestor in a miserable plight. It is impossible for you to save them any more than it is possible to change history. The Ubh is in that state in Tir Andoman because that was how they were in life. Their real self has long since departed and may have had many lives since, it may or may not be leaving similar scenarios in Tir Andoman, but that is really up to it. Your only responsibility is that your part of the Song does not end in such a sorry state. You will have left countless miserable scenes in Tir Andoman yourself in your various lives, indeed you may even be looking at one of your old ones.

---

[3] Some of the barrows that were shut down still contain ambassadors. But these are the result of the rise of the neo-pagan movement in modern times. The West Kennett barrow has an old one and he informed me that he was called back to the barrow after many centuries in Tir Andoman to answer the needs of new worshippers. Although his bones were long gone from the Barrow he had managed to stay strong because of the magnetism of the nearby Avebury Stone circle, the offerings left behind by worshippers and the energy left behind by some of their rites.

In your initial dealings with the Ancestors, you should speak through the Cucullati until you have some experience. They may also be called upon to act as your defenders if one of the dead becomes angry with you.

Injuries that happen in Tir Andoman will never prove fatal in Bith, but it is possible that you will be unwell for a time while thy Ubh recovers.

Of the Emerald Heart of the Earth

As we have said the Emerald Heart of the Earth resides in the centre of Tir Andoman. It has no real physical place in Bith but has an association with the Earth's heart. It is the indwelling of the Song within the physical structure of the Earth and is the size of the World of Bith itself. It may only be seen in Tir Andoman, for it makes no physical appearance in Bith or Mag Mor, except in times of deep spiritual awakening, otherwise it remains occult residing in Tir Andoman.

Its nature is to empower one's life destiny, but also to remember the past. Thus the long forgotten dead and the Gods and Goddesses are maintained by its energy. It shall be your task throughout your work in Druidry to continually seek this Emerald, for with it you shall gain much magical power and healing. It will give you wisdom and understanding and reveal your true destiny.

However, once the Emerald Heart is found in one part of Tir Andoman, it will move and need to be found again. Once it is seen in one form it will take another. This is because it is the embodiment of Amhran that is always changing and adapting.[4]

One should not consider the elusive nature of Amhran frustrating for the act of questing for it in the Three Worlds is thy true calling as a Druid. The process of searching unlocks the secrets of creation and nature and will enable you to be a true reflection for the Oinacos.

---

[4] I always felt that the Quest for the Emerald Heart of the World was similar to that of the Holy Grail. I was heartened in this view when I read the version of the legend written by Christian leTroyes where the Grail was described as a green stone that always changed.

The Pendragons

In the centre of Tir Andoman is a green emerald, which is the heart of the Earth. This is the source where the Amhran is centred in Earth. This energy flows through the earth through the two poles which when seen by those with the Sight, appear to be dragons. On the North Pole is mounted the White Pendragon and on the Antipodes is the Red Pendragon. Through this force is the Amhran mediated throughout the three-fold earth. The White Pendragon is attributed to fire and at certain times of year when the White Pendragon power is strong his white light will be divided in the extreme Northern sky so that it shows as a rainbow of colour. The South Pole is attributed to water and the Mather.

The Pendragons move in cycles and during various times of the year one holds sway over the other. In Spring and Summer the White Dragon is dominant and during the Autumn and Winter the Red Dragon holds more power. When the seasons change from winter to spring and from autumn to winter is the time of balance. You, who are tuned to nature, will be aware of this period for it is a moment when the Amhran pauses before changing his tempo.

Each nation, having a common ancestry, partakes of a different cycle sometimes leaning to the Red and at other times to the White Pendragon. All men in that nation are subject to the same fluctuation and at certain crisis points there is a tendency towards discord. This discord resolves some issue and then harmony is restored. The nation now called England has periods of crisis at a point between 23 to 26 years.[5] Some of this discord is resolved unseen by the world's rulers and the dangers by-passed while others are not and discord reigns.

A Man tendeth to favour one Pendragon over another. Those with many Wanderers in Air and Fire signs favour the White Pendragon while those of Water and Earth favour the Red.

In our rites we draw up the Red and White Pendragons and to use this pure energy to bring about what we wish. When we strike the ground with our single staffs we are attempting to draw

---

[5] Some work we did on the Pendragon cycles of America seem to suggest a similar cycle in that country only some two years behind. France is about a year ahead and Russia about two.

Red and White Pendragon energy up them to create a ball of pure white light on top of them. This white light can be seen by those with the Sight and heard as a pure note by those with the Hearing. With our hands on our staff we direct the energy into a form that we wish by using a rhyme, poem or song which encapsulates our wish.

This rhyme is repeated until the Pendragon energy gives the words life. Once living the words will rebound throughout Tir Andoman and gather the allies they need to burst forth upon Bith as thy desire.

In the first degree the Red and White Pendragon are seen as providing a gateway between Bith and Tir Andoman and Tir Andoman and Mag Mor. This is because, when the Pendragon energy is separated it createth a vortex in between itself and this forges a portal between this world and the Tir Andoman.

In the body of a Man the ball of each foot connects energy to a cauldron at the groin. From this point, the Pendragons snake around the staff of the spine meeting at the heart and the brow. The heads then extend out of the head like horns and turn to face each other. When a Druid draweth power up his body as part of a rite his body becometh like his staff and a bright ball of light appeareth between the horns. This is illustrated by the position of Creation where the Druid stands with his arms representing the Pendragons pointing towards the Orb of Light above his head.

The cauldron at the groin is attributed to the Mather and Tir Andoman. The cauldron at the heart is attributed to the Amhran and Bith and the Brow is the Ather, or Mag Mor.

In the ordinary man the Spark of the Oinacos sleeps in the Heart. However when it is awoken it grows like an oak tree sending roots to the groin and a trunk to the brow. During the rising of the Pendragon, the Spark of the One rises bathed in the Song from the emerald heart of the world and the Three are One again.[6]

---

[6] Man becomes most like a God and God is riding in a Chariot.

Practicing the Pendragon

Thou shalt perform this exercise at least once a day save when the Moon is dark.

With thy feet on the floor and standing upright, imagine a green emerald in the centre of the earth. This point shall be deep beneath thy feet, with the Pendragons coiled around bathed in the light of the emerald. Take a deep breath thrice. Then in thy fantasy seeth the Pendragons uncoil and rise up so that the Red is under the ball of thy left foot and the White is under the ball of thy right.

Singeth the following AAAA OOOO in the correct notes of the letters alternating in a cycle as the serpents coil up each leg. As they they meet in thy groin, feel a burst of light and, in thy fantasy formeth it unto a Silver cauldron of greenish light.

Sing the the following note:

OOOOOOOOOOOOOOOOOOOOO.

Then allow them to coil up the spine as thou singest AAAA alternating with OOOOO again until the heads meet again in the breast. Thou should feeleth a burst of light and see spontaneously a golden caldron of energy forming.

Singeth thou:

UUUUUUUUUUUUUUUUUUUUU

Then alloweth the serpents again to coil further up thy spine as thou singest AAAA alternating with OOOOO until the heads meet again at the brow. Thou should feeleth a burst of light and see spontaneously a glass cauldron of energy forming.

Sing:

AAAAAAAAAAAAAAAAAAAA

Then allow them to rise up out of thy skull as thou singest AAAA alternating with OOOOO again so that thou art crowned with the Pendragons as horns. On your Right shall be the White Dragon and on your Left the Red. Between them all see a bright white ball of light.

Sing with the correct notes:

AAAA, OOOO, UUUU

Thou willst have a great feeling of exaltation and power and will feel the tree of the Oinacos grow within thee.

Of this most excellent of exercises

Be aware that the drawing of Pendragon power through thy body in the manner, which is described, will purify thine Ubh and empower the flame that surroundeth it. But be wary for the Pendragons do empower the very discord that dwelleth in thy breast and in thy loins. For the force of the Pendragon is blind and any creatures of discord that dwell within thee will beg thine attention immediately.

Such creatures will approach thee in the guise of divers images usually of thine own transgressions and shortcomings. One should confess these to thy self lest they gain power over thee. Then thou shalt establish which note they are a discord of. If thou art troubled by unmerited hatred or malice towards some man thou should work with the note of Mars until the discord is tuned to its correct note. If thou art troubled by a fear of death then this shall be a discord of the true note of Saturn etc.

The words here are a little obscure so I shall endeavour to clarify what they are suggesting. In modern psychological terms the drawing up of the Pendragon force powers up the entire personality and this includes what Freud called the ID and Carl Jung called the Shadow. Included in these parts of the self are the neurotic behaviour that we get from living in the world; they are the dark side of ourselves which we usually keep locked up so we don't rush out and behave in a manner that might get us arrested or shunned by polite society. What this little missive is suggesting is that these shadows are simply true notes of the song, which have become corrupted by discord. The Pendragon exercise brings these discords to the surface and enables us to cure them. It is not simply a matter of humming the right note either. What you should do is allow the shadow to appear and look at why you think and feel this way. 'Humming the correct note' while you do this process will speed up the healing process. It does this because it acknowledges that each of these little shadows are actually part of the real you that has become unbalanced. A hatred of a person might have its roots in a justifiable injury that you had suffered early in your life but, never having been resolved properly, has appeared as a discord. Repairing the discord in your life is an important part of the second degree, which is all about the occult sides of your self.

(C Robertson)

Of the Entering of the Tir Andoman

It is the work of this grade to start exploring Tir Andoman. To understand how we do this one must start to see that the imagination is the tool which Amhran used to create the three-fold world so that it would be a mirror to Oinacos. This imagination is part of the magic of the Amhran.

When we use our imagination, we are using the Amhran's powers within us to see into the portals of Tir Andoman. Our initial forays into that land will only reach as far as our personal world. We see our own world coloured by the light of our own wisdom. This is what is called daydreaming and has little merit. However the deeper we go into this land the less subjective our vision becomes.

Using a rite to focus our attention beyond our limited view of Tir Andoman enhances this process. To do this you should make a stave out of Apple and another of Hazel. This should be made in the traditional manner by approaching the Tree and requesting that a sacrifice be made for thine entry into Tir Andoman. These staves need not be as tall as the Pendragon staves we use in the meetings, but you should be able to walk underneath them. Above them you should lash a lintel that should be made of the wood of the zodiac sign of thy birth. Upon it should be carved the letters of the word

Tir Andoman in Ogham and the first and last letters of your name. You should also buy yourself the skin of a calf which is large enough for you to lie upon.

Set aside the space in the traditional manner and place the calfskin in the centre. Either hammer the doorway into the ground in the north of the space or lean it against a wall.[7]

Take the staff of apple in both hands at about half way and say:

I call unto the Emerald Heart of the World
I call unto thee Red Pendragon of the Mather
Rise Up
Rise Up
Rise Up I say
Indwell in this token of thy power
As I call thee by thy note.

Sing the note of the Mather until the Pendragon has risen to the top of the Apple Staff.

OOOOOOOOOOOOOOOO

Take the staff of Hazel in both hands at about half way and say:

I call unto the Emerald Heart of the World
I call unto thee White Pendragon of the Ather
Rise Up
Rise Up
Rise Up I say
Indwell in this token of thy power
As I call thee by thy note.

Sing the note of the Ather until the Pendragon has risen to the top of the Hazel Staff.

AAAAAAAAAAAAAAAA

Stand in the Position of Power leaning on your own personal staff

I who am half man and half tree

---

[7] I used to prop mine up against the wall of my cave. I know of another Druid who used to hammer his into the beach of a Welsh lake where the water met the land.

> *I who have my feet on the ground and can touch the sky.*
> *I who am a creature of flaming water*
> *I who am in a place that is no-where and everywhere*
> *Open this Portal unto Tir Andoman.*

You should see a vortex open in the shape of an ellipse. Lie on the calf's skin and then in your mind's eye walk through the portal. You will find that the doorway can be summoned to anywhere in Tir Andoman by standing in the Position of Power leaning on the Other world equivalent of your staff and saying.

> *I who am half man and half tree*
> *I who have my feet on the ground and can touch the sky.*
> *I who am a creature of flaming water*
> *I who am in a place that is no-where and everywhere*
> *Open this Portal unto Bith.*

Now immediately upon thine entrance into Tir Andoman thou should call Cucullati. When thou crosseth the threshold if they are not waiting for you thou shouldest call for them. By standing in the position of Power and saying:

> *I who am half man and half tree*
> *I who have my feet on the ground and can touch the sky.*
> *I who am a creature of flaming water*
> *I who am in a place that is no-where and everywhere*
> *Request the help of the Cucullati of Tir Andoman.*

If they fail to appear then return for it is not thy time to enter Tir Andoman.

Upon your return, rise from thy bed and take thy iron dagger and say:

> *"Let any creature of Tir Andoman who may have followed me into Bith return to his kingdom in the name of the Amhran I command thee."*

Wait a while and then stand in the Position of Power as before say:

> *I who am half man and half tree*
> *I who have my feet on the ground and can touch the sky.*

> *I who am a creature of flaming water*
> *I who am in Bith*
> *Close this Portal to Tir Andoman.*

Stand with you right hand on the Hazel Staff and your Left on the Apple Staff for a moment and then draw your hands together so that they clasp shut.

Of the Rites of Protection

Of a house

Take thou dagger of iron and go unto the most Eastern part of thy dwelling. Dip thy knife into wine and draw the Ogham rune for the Ather. Sing his note. Walk to the most Southern part of thy dwelling dip thy knife into wine and repeat this act. Do so again in the East.

Sheath thy blade and take up thy staff. Stand thou in the Position of Power and say:

> *I who am half man and half tree*
> *I who have my feet on the ground and can touch the sky.*
> *I who am a creature of flaming water*
> *I who am in a place that is no-where*
> *and everywhere say verily that*
> *In the name of Ather and with blood and with Iron I seal this house in flames.*
> *I bind all who would do me harm in this place turn aside.*
> *Iron and Blood shall stand against thee in Bith*
> *Iron and Blood shall stand against thee in Tir Andoman*
> *Iron and Blood shall stand against thee in Mag Mor*
> *Iron and Blood shall stand against thee from Sunrise unto Sunset*
> *Iron and Blood shall stand against thee from Sunset unto Sunrise*
> *Iron and Blood shall stand against thee from the now*
> *Iron and Blood shall stand against thee until the Amhran finishes the Singing.*

Stand in the centre of the house in the Position of Power and say.

I who am half man and half tree
I who have my feet on the ground and can touch the sky.
I who am a creature of flaming water
I who am in a place that is no-where and everywhere.
Say verily that the blessing of the Amhran hath descended upon this place
Let it be a place of peace
Let it be a place of refuge
Let it be a place of inspiration
Let it be a place of rest
Let it be a place of study
Let it be free from discord
From now until the Amhran finishes the Singing.

To protect thy land

Take four large iron nails or spikes and on the night after the night of the new moon go unto the furthest East of thy property. Take one of the Spikes and hold it upwards in the Position of Power.

I who am half man and half tree
I who have my feet on the ground and can touch the sky.
I who am a creature of flaming water
I who am in a place that is no-where and everywhere.
Say verily that the blessing of the Amhran hath descended upon this creature of Iron.

Sing the note of the Amhran

UUUUUUUUUUUU
Let no being seen or unseen
In the Air
On the Ground
Or Below
Of Mag Mor
Of Tir Andoman
Of Bith
Pass thee by

*Spirit of Iron thou art the guardian of this place.
If they would do me or mine harm
Let them pass not.*

Drive the spike deep into the Earth and then pour wine over the top.

By this sacrifice Spirit of Iron thou art wedded unto the Earth to guard the land from attack from the East.

Repeat this in the South, West and North. Then go unto the centre of thy land and stand in the position of Power.

*I who am half man and half tree
I who have my feet on the ground and can touch the sky.
I who am a creature of flaming water
I who am in a place that is no-where and everywhere.
Say verily that the blessing of the Amhran hath descended upon this place
Let it be a place of peace
Let it be a place of refuge
Let it be a place of inspiration
Let it be a place of rest
Let it be a place of study
Let it be free from discord
From now until the Amhran finishes the Singing.*

Of a person

The Druid's egg given at initiation should be more than enough for anyone, but occasionally someone who is not of the Order will ask for some sort of magical protection. Generally this should be declined as many who seek such protection are generally subject to their own paranoid delusions. This rite is for those cases that are not. It is also effective in healing those who suffer from debilitating illnesses that are caused by a weakness or leakage from the Ubh.

After thou hast been requested for aid thrice, request that the person go into nature and find a smooth round rock the size of an egg. On the night after the new moon tell the person to sleep (or relax as deeply as possible) set aside thy sacred space in the ancient manner. Draw the first and last letters of the person's name in Ogham on the stone. Then stand in the Position of Power and say:

> *I who am half man and half tree*
> *I who have my feet on the ground and can touch the sky.*
> *I who am a creature of flaming water*
> *I who am in a place that is no-where and everywhere*
> *Call into this place the Ubh of Flame of* [Insert the full name of the person]
> *Come into this place between worlds and dwell in this stone.*
> *Come by the three-fold request they have made.*

You should see a spirit of flame arriving into the circle and pouring itself into the stone. When this has happened go to the East take the stone in thy left hand and thy Staff in thy right and say:-

> *Spirits of Air strengthen this Ubh of Fire so that it mayest become a rock against the arrows of the enemy.*

Go to the South take the stone in thy left hand and thy Staff in thy right and say:-

> *Spirits of Fire strengthen this Ubh of Fire so that it mayest become a rock against the arrows of the enemy.*

Go unto the West and repeat with the spirits of Water and in the North with the Spirits of Earth. Then take the stone unto the centre of thy space and say to the Ubh of Flame in the stone:

> *By the Power of the Ather*
> *By the Rays of the Sun*
> *I bind thee and [name of the person] together*
> *So that Amhran and the Singer*
> *Become One.*
> *Stone shall you be*
> *Strong shall you be*
> *None shall shatter thee.*

Place the Stone on the ground. See the Pendragons coiled around the Emerald Heart of the Earth. Smite the ground with thy staff in a rhythm of thine own invention until thou seest the Pendragons uncoil and rise upwards coiling about thy staff until they form horns above the top of it. Place the stone between the horns and say:

> *With the powers of the Emerald Heart of the Earth*
> *I renew the Ubh of* [insert full name of person].
> *No longer a weak Ubh, hath he* (or she)
> *But a flaming rock from the centre of the Earth.*
> *Let these powers fuse and be so in Bith*
> *As I chant the three fold name.*

Chant *AOU* until thou seeth the rock blaze with flame.

Wrap the rock in a cloth of chequered colours. Thou mayst give it to the person to be placed in a safe place or buried in the earth where none shall find it.

To divine the person who would ill-wish thee

Take a beetle and place it in a cup. Turn the cup over and draw a circle of about a hand span in diameter about it. Say:-

> *In the name of the Amhran*
> *Creature that scuttles reveal unto me who would do*
> [insert name of victim] *harm.*
> *Show me where the person lives.*

Raise the bowl and the beetle will move towards a direction. At the point that the beetle crosses the circumference of the circle the attacker is in that direction. If the beetle moves not, or fails to cross the circumference of the circle after a minute then either no attack is coming, or the rite is unable to locate it. Likewise if the beetle flees so fast that it cannot be recaptured then that is a portent that thou has no business in this rite.

Replace the beetle in the cup and draw another circle. Say:-

> *In the name of the Amhran*
> *Creature that scuttles reveal unto me who would do*

[insert name of victim] *harm.*
Show me the sex of the person.

If the beetle moves to the right the person is male, if it is to the left it is female. If the beetle fails to move then the act is the work of several persons. If it flees it has told thee enough.

Replace the beetle in the cup and draw another circle. This time place the letters evenly around the circle and say:-

In the name of the Amhran
Creature that scuttles reveal unto me who would do
[insert name of victim] *harm.*
Show me the person [or ringleader's] *name.*

The beetle will move to the letter of the person. This shall be their first name. If the beetle fails to move or flees it has told thee enough. This may be repeated so that it shows the surname of the person but no further.

When thou hast finished thank the beetle and set it free with the blessing of Amhran.

Approaching the Gods

When journeying in Tir Andoman you will encounter Gods and Goddesses in their realms. Usually long before you meet them you will encounter the Ubhs of their most loyal worshippers. To such Ubhs to commune with their God or Goddess is the ultimate reward for a life of devotion. They will exhibit some surprise that one who does not follow their religion shall be in this place and will often mistake you for an emissary from another God.

Remember that but for their devotion they are no different from any other ancestor who may be dwelling elsewhere in Tir Andoman and must be treated as such. They are extremely unlikely to have a trace of the Oinacos in them unless some pathology has been allowed to develop.

The Gods and Goddesses will dwell in a scene that is appropriate to their mythos and will often be in the process of enacting out the legends. They must be extremely carefully approached as they have much power, which has been granted, to them by their followers in some cases over Eons. In the cosmic hierarchy they are much below thee as they lack the Oinacos, but never the less they could do thee much harm if they are not treated with diplomacy.

When you first appear in Tir Andoman it is best to let Cucullati speak for you. As you gain in experience you will become aware what is safe and what is not.

Be aware that you will encounter many Gods and Goddesses that you hast never heard of before, or discover that they have names that are unfamiliar to you. This is because some of them are long forgotten and their rites on earth long past and others who are recalled by history are more likely to be remembered in Tir Andoman by the names given by their worshippers rather than historians.

Like any being in Tir Andoman do not eat with them. If they offer gifts make sure that they are not conditional upon anything that resembles worship. Worship not Cucullati even though they may appear to save thy life on many occasions.

Of the Animal Spirits

Animals are creatures of Amhran who mostly lack the spark of Oinacos. Upon their death their Ubh of Flame merge into a single entity that represents their species. Thus all dogs merge into the part of Amhran who corresponds to the Great Dog and all Magpies merge into the Great Magpie. A spark of the Oinacos who vieweth the species through their eyes ennobles these Great Beings.

At times an animal develops a degree of individuality such that the Oinacos in the Great Being decides to allow it to be reborn so that it may experience something that is like unto itself. After a time these animals are permitted to be indwelled by a human Ubh of which has yet to walk upon the earth. After several lives living as an animal the human then is given a human body. However they never forget their animal life which shapes the way the Song will develop in later life. Often they will have strong associations with that particular animal and in later legends they would forbid themselves from eating the meat of that particular animal. They will find interaction with members of that species much easier because they instinctively know its language. Some people, such as the horse whisperers, are able to use this knowledge to train or raise the animals from whom they are descended.

Not all pass through an animal stage but it is extremely common. These are the animals a human is likely to have been. Many of these are domesticated, this is because of their close contact with humans makes them susceptible to becoming individual:-

    Hawk
    Eagle
    Crow
    Wolf
    Dog
    Cat[7]
    Rat
    Mouse
    Rabbit
    Deer
    Chicken
    Pig
    Cattle
    Horse
    Pony
    Donkey
    Salmon
    Whale
    Dolphin
    Badger
    Snake
    Bear
    Otter

To find out which animal from which you are descended thou should enter Tir Andoman and approach the Cucullati. Ask them to take you to a place where you can meet the Great Animal from which you descended. If they agree they will take you to field, or Grove

---

[7] This was not on the original list, probably because it was a later arrival in the British Isles, but I have encountered people who have associations with Cats.

or similar environment. There may be many animals in this place but your animal ancestor will approach you. You will be able to communicate after a fashion and will not need the Cucullati to act as a mediator. From it you will relearn of the lessons of the species that are deep within you. Afterwards renew your experience with the animal

Rite of animal working
by CR

Preparation

In either a clean clear room or outdoors walk out a circle to mark your sacred space. Saying:

> *Let the Mather enclose this sacred space, as she encloses the whole of creation. May this circumference be the lip of her sacred cauldron, that all living creatures dwell.*

Then go to the East of your circle and start walking clockwise around your circle getting closer to the centre of your sacred space saying:

> *I walk the sacred spiral from Without to Within, symbolising the great Quest from where all journeys begin and from where they proceed.*

Measure your heartbeat and time it to your breath. Relax into the rhythm of your breathing. Relax deeper into trance. Feel yourself sinking into the roots of the Earth. In your mind's eye face East and mentally call out:

> *I send out a call to that Animal spirit who consents to be my guide. May my call be heard on the Eastern Wind and draw it to this place.*

You face South and say:

> *I send out a call to that Animal spirit who consents to be my guide. May my call be heard on the Southern Wind and draw it to this place.*

Now face West and say:

I send out a call to that Animal spirit who consents to be my guide. May my call be heard on the Western Wind and draw it to this place.

Now face North and say:

I send out a call to that Animal spirit who consents to be my guide. May my call be heard on the Northern Wind and draw it to this place.

You return to face East:

In the names of the Mather may the Winds of the World carry my call to my animal guide, bring it to me so that I would understand the Song of the Animals.

There will be a pause. If nothing happens then your animal guide does not wish to speak to you at the moment. However after a while, if you are lucky, a creature will come to you. At this point simply introduce yourself to your guide and tell it about yourself. Then ask it for a name by which to call it. An image will pop into your mind. It will be the first image that comes into your head.

Once you have exchanged names and communed for a while visualise yourself saying good-bye and ascending into Bith.

When you have done this say:-

The journey is complete now I return from Within to Without bringing the light of knowledge with me.

Walk the circle anti-clockwise.

I have partaken of the cauldron of Wisdom, the Mather has led me from darkness to light now the hidden universe shall dwell on the earth through me. So mote it be!

The work

For the next few weeks you should meditate on your guide and what it means to you. You should supplement this with scientific study on the animal, to learn about its life cycle, habitat and function in the great wheel of life.

Then when you are ready, repeat the ritual above and call your guide by its name. If it does not attend then it is not ready to teach you and more study is required. (This study simulates the time that the Druid would spend studying the animal and sometimes this was quite some years).

If it appears then talk to it respectfully and ask to learn its mysteries. In your mind's eye allow yourself to change into the shape of the creature. Make yourself slightly bigger than the creature. Feel what it is like to move as it moves and see the world from its perspective.

Then, when you and the creature are ready, step over the creature and allow it to partially merge with you. Your bodies should be one, but your mind should be separate.

After this has been achieved make mind-to-mind contact with the spirit guide. This will hit you like a rush of power and may force you to break contact. It takes time to master this and it should not be rushed. Then when you feel you have it mastered allow yourself to roam the other world landscape with your guide — doing as it does.

Be prepared to be shocked. I know of a number of animal lovers who have struggled from the experience to tell of their horror (and the feelings of joy from their animal guides) of eating a particularly gruesome bug. Then there was the vegetarian who lived through the savage killing, disembowelling and eating of a baby bear when she was a timber wolf or person who was one with Owl as she flew from a tree and expertly slit the throat of a small stoat. Nature is raw in tooth and claw — it is not nice. But then again these things are within us and need to be explored.

Shapeshifting

Now, you will have heard tales of Druids that turned themselves into animals for the purposes of spying on their enemies, hiding, or in some cases fighting. There is some truth to these tales but they should not be taken literally.

Druids can create an Athdhold or shape shifted form from their own Ubh of Fire using the technique below, they may then shift part of their awareness to this form. It may then travel through the world of Bith as the creature that the form resembles. Such a form may be seen by those gifted with the Sight but will remain invisible to the profane.

But in such a circumstances the Druid's physical body remains in a trance in another location and as such is unchanged by the action of shape shifting.

An Athdhold requires some degree of competence. To learn how to use it correctly as one needs some knowledge of the animal one is shifting unto. Thus he who would fly in the form of a bird must know the action of the wings and tail feathers.

For this reason, it is better for one to chose an animal that one has already been, as the lessons of movement will be much quicker. Also the effort of building a form that can move through Bith effectively requires so much time and effort that a Druid will only chose an animal to fly, an animal to run and an animal to swim. Those that are proficient at creating such forms will also create an animal to burrow.

One must dedicate much time to the study of the animal, namely its movement, feeding and mating patterns. Many Druids keep such animals as pets so that they can become familiar with their form.

The creation of a form is done as part of a rite that rarely needs to be repeated as the form of the animal is absorbed into the Druid's Ubh of Fire and can be recreated at will.

The Rite of creation of an Athdhold

Take thou twigs of apple, hazel and fir trees to build a fire. Set aside the place as in thine normal custom.

Perform the exercise of the raising of the Pendragon.

Add the green wood of the apple and grass so that it createth a dark smoke. In thy mind's eye see the Ubh of Fire about thee, stand in the position of Creation. Then taketh that fire and project a bubble of it into the smoke so that it floats in the smoke and is joined to thy body with a thread.

Shape the bubble into the clearest likeness of the animal thou wish. The smoke will assist thee and will become the material component of the creature.

Lie down and relax as much as possible, breath out and then shift your awareness along the thread and into the head of the animal. Command the eyes of the animal to open so that you are seeing with its eyes. Command the ears of the animal to open so that you hear with its ears. Command the nose of the animal to open so that you may smell with its nose. Command the surface of the animal to become sensitive so that you may touch with its body.

Then thou should name the animal by having it say:

I am the Athdhold of the Druid (insert Order name)
When he is my spark of life I am known as (insert thine
name for the creature)

Move the animal from the fire and start its journey where thou would.

All that is required to return is to think of thine body and the cord that joins thee shall instantly tighten and you shall be back. If you art unable to get back into thy body just imagine opening the eyes of your body and breathing. The Athdhold will simply merge into thine Ubh of Fire and will be able to be separated by an act of will on the second or subsequent occasions. If thou would shape shift then set aside thy space, lie down and relax. Breath out and say the name of thine creature. It will then fly out from thine Ubh of flame. Take another breath and move thy self into it.

Enter not into Tir Andoman in this form as thou wilt not have protection of the Order in this form which is stripped of thine initiation tokens.

Note that it is not meet to remain too long in the form of a beast as after time you will take on the part of the Song that the animal responds to. It is not meet to remain longer than a night and a day in this form as not only will thine own body start to be weakened by the activity, but thine own mind will become beast like.

Of Dew

Dew is the water of the Moon and is placed by the Mather as a blessing upon the land. It may be collected to use as blessed water of cleansing and is even more efficacious than water from a sacred well.

It is best harvested on the Beltane moon as the virtue contained at that time is so much the greater.

Of Divination

There are many different methods of foreshadowing the future yet all have their weaknesses and strengths. This is not because the techniques are unreliable, but rather that the ability of the Druids to interpret what they see is always coloured. When you use a technique to foreshadow or predict events you are watching through your Ubh of flame. This contains perceptions and memories and associations that are unique to you and therefore also reflect your prejudices. Thus one man who sees a raven in a skrying mirror might foretell of death, however another might see it as an omen of regeneration. Now this is all very well, as you could simply say, well, I will use this language of symbols so that it is in accord with what I think. However, this too is fraught with inconsistency. You will be unaware that you have any particular association with many of the symbols that you will see. You will be aware of situations where you have awoken from a strange dream that you have been unable to understand because the images seemed too obscure. Sometimes in contemplation or upon asking another for an interpretation you can unlock some measure of the dream. During your long work with this Order you will start to understand much of the system of tokens that resides in your head you will also be taught by tree, animal, men and Gods what each symbol means. Note them well when you are taught and if necessary write them in a book. This would be a lexicon to your own symbolic system. Here is an example of some written from my own book:-

> Crow - wisdom, understanding and death
> Oak shoot - new history begins
> Oak tree - stability, history, future, death
> Light Rain - blessing of the Ather, new beginnings
> Storm clouds - Discord

Now if I am skrying into a pool of water for another and see the following:-

There are storm clouds and a crow settles onto an oak tree which starts to shoot forth new leaves. Instead of a storm there is a light rain.

Thus it would be possible to interpret what I see as:-

There are many problems in your life at the moment, arguments and depression. But I see that change is coming. There will be a period of sudden unpleasantness that will enable something new to begin. Your life will not be swept away, just that it will begin again from where it left off before this darkness happened. Something new and promising will be offered which you should decide to follow.

Of the Question

In Divination and indeed all aspects of thy dealings with creatures on all three worlds it is vital that the Druid know what question he (or she) needs to ask. The entire mythology of the Order is based on the premise that Oinacos started the process of creation by asking questions.

A question has a magical power all of its own. The moment it is created then it shouts out to the rest of creation for an answer. Amhran demands that once a question had been framed then eventually an answer has to be found.

Thus framing your questions must be done with care and be as specific as possible. No question should ever be able to be simply answered yes or no. These answers give no development to the Amhran and are just statements.

> Questions that begin with *how* giveth instructions.
> Questions that begin with *who* giveth the names of people or Gods.
> Questions that begin with *what* giveth the names of things or animals.
> Questions that begin with *when* giveth the location in time.
> Questions that begin with *where* giveth the location in space
> Questions that begin with *why* are the most powerful questions of all.
> They are what provides a true mirror to this time and place
> They create change.
> They reveal the future.

Of the predictive methods

Always eat hazel nuts before commencing divination, it will aid thy sight. A person who would enhance their ability to see should, once in their life, place the drops of green rowan juice in their eyes. This juice should be diluted with dew; one drop of juice for nine drops of dew.

Hydromancy

Takest thou a cauldron of black iron and fill it with water either taken from rain or from a sacred spring or lake. Purify it as thou wast taught then leave it to reflect the full moon for a night. Then place a drop of blood or wine into the cauldron and cover it until thou art ready.

Set aside thy space in the traditional manner and rest with the cauldron on thy lap. While looking into the water say the following:
I ask the question
Creature of Mather
Reveal the Song.

Chant the following nine times:

Let Amhran be revealed

Then sing the Note of Amhran

UUUUUUUUUUUUUUUUUU

Now allow thine eyes to go soft (ie out of focus). After a while the water shall cloud over and figures and shapes shall form. When this happens ask thy question.

The water shall last 13 days if it drieth not up. Then it should be returned to either a river or spring.

Pyromancy

Prepare twigs from an oak and an apple tree. Tie them in three large bundles with hemp. Place them so that thou wouldst form a pyramid. Place a candle underneath and surround it with straw. Surround the entire fire with a circle of wine or bull's blood.

Prepare thy space in the ancient manner with the wood in the centre. Light the candle so that the straw catches afire and from there the rest of the bundles. When the fire hath taken. Cast in it holly, oak and apple leaves.

I ask the question
Creature of Ather
Reveal the Song.

Chant the following nine times:

Let Amhran be revealed

Then sing the Note of Amhran

UUUUUUUUUUUUUUUUUU

Now allow thine eyes to go soft (ie out of focus). After thou shalt see different shapes in the fire.

Oreanaireacht
(Divination by flights of birds)

Prepare thy circle in the ancient manner upon a site where thou hast clear vision to the North, South, East and West. Commune as much as you can with the force of the area.

When thou hast finished, face East and say:

I ask the question
Creatures of Ather
Reveal the Song.

Chant the following nine times:

Let Amhran be revealed

Then sing the Note of Amhran

UUUUUUUUUUUUUUUUUU

As the note of Amhran passeth note any birds that may be seen. If thou seeth none within thrice turning about clockwise the song shall not be revealed unto you at this time.

If there are birds in the East: good fortune in terms of what the questioner wants in accordance to the number thou seeth.
If there are birds in the South: good fortune is starting to ebb away but is strong at the present in terms of what the questioner wants in accordance to the number thou seeth.
If there are birds in the West: bad Fortune in terms of what the questioner wants in accordance to the number thou seeth.
If there are birds in the North: bad Fortune starteth to improve in terms of what the questioner wants in accordance to the number thou seeth.

Note then the direction that the birds thou has seen are moving towards. This is the direction that the fates are moving the person towards. Thus birds that start in the North moving to the East show that a bleak situation will get better while the same birds moving towards the North will indicate that while things seem to be getting better they will soon become still more bleak.

Numbers of birds are important - the greater the number the stronger the tide in relation to the question. If several stay still or go in an opposite direction from others then it indicates that there are several courses that a man may follow. He should go towards the point where the greater number of birds travelled, even if this should take him to the North or West.

Two or more flocks of birds coming together is a sign that many forces shall be marshalled to bring about a matter for good or ill.

Birds that fly overhead indicate that the matter will soon be resolved. Sounds of birds either coming from the direction thou art looking, or from another direction should also be taken into account as if thou were watching that quarter.

Different species of birds mean different things thus:

Blackbird: secrets
Crane: stillness, birth and death
Crows: death, war, magic
Ducks: dreams, communication, flexibility.
Eagle: the forces of Mag Mor
Geese: war, defence, Tir Andoman.
Gulls: the forces of Tir Andoman
Hawk: meditation followed by action
Magpies: theft, writing and law
Owl (by day): ill omen, spirits of the dead
Pigeon: stupidity, adaptability and love.
Rooks: wisdom
Sparrows and tits: industry and work
Starlings: groups, dramas, mimicry
Swallows: travel and journeys
Swans: love, commitment, silence

Many different types of birds in the sector indicate that there are many different issues related to the question (usually of the nature of the types of birds).

Birds rising suddenly from a tree or landing upon one indicates something connected with the meaning of that tree ie Oak would mean Saturn. Everything should be interpreted in the order that it happens.

Examples

I ask a question about my wife who is ill. I look at the east: there is nothing there. I look to the South and West, there is nothing. In the North a flock of Starlings are heading towards the East. A group of seven sparrows rise up from an old yew tree and I can hear the quacking of a duck in the distance. I interpret this thus:

My wife is getting better and indeed the only reason that she is not completely better is that after such a long time being unwell she is used to it. She needs to get more activity and to become more interested in life again. We need to talk about this issue. My job is miserable and I am waiting to hear of the results of an application for another post.

Nothing is visible in the East, or South but in the West a large group of (unknown) birds flocks together and splits with the greater part of them heading towards the North and a lesser group heading towards the West. A small sparrow darts close by and I hear a pigeon flap behind me.

It is unlikely that I am going to get the job although my employment situation is about to get better where I am, if I continue to work hard and make the best of it for a time.

Geomancy

Collect seven black pebbles and seven white ones and either a green stone of Iona or a marble of glass. Mark a black and white pebble for each symbol of the Wanderer. Chant the note of the Wanderer over each until the symbol glows with power.

Prepare they circle in the ancient manner upon a site of bare earth. Then take thy staff and draw a circle with thyself in the centre. Divide the circle into twelve and place Aries in the first house and so on widdershins about the circle.

When thou hast finished face East say:

I ask the question
Creatures of Mather
Reveal the Song.

Chant the following nine times:

Let Amhran be revealed

Then sing the Note of Amhran:

UUUUUUUUUUUUUUUUUUU

While thinking of the Question place the 15 stones on your head and allow them to fall where they willst.

The White stones indicate the positive aspects of the Wanderers whilst the black are the discordant ones.

The ascendant indicates the querent. Only look at the houses that pertain to thine question. The glass ball represents Amhran. It indicates where destiny is focused in the querent's life at the present. If it falls on a house related to the question it indicates that the issue is crucial and must be resolved as part of the Song of the person. Such issues must not be left to resolve themselves, but will require some action on the part of the querent.

Of the uses of the Magical positions

The Druid is given two positions in which to stand when casting magic. The first, and most often used is the position of power. This is used in all general rites where thou art seeking to represent thyself as a being of power. Energy generated by this position is projected from the right hand. An adaptation of this position is when the right hand is used to open either the left and or the right eye. This position is used to focus the energy of the Druid still further. If it is toward the right eye, the energy is drawn towards the Mather and if it is the right then it is towards the Ather. You may hear that the Druids used to use these positions to either bless (left eye) or curse (right eye) but again like many legends it only shows part of the tale.

The second position is the position of creation that is used when one wishes to bring something new into creation. It is used during the first-degree rite to create new forms within the candidate's Ubh. It would also be used if you were creating shapeshifted forms or other sorts of creatures out of thine own Ubh. It is also used when healing another's Ubh of Fire and other acts that directly involve the activation of the Pendragon force.

Rite of healing discord

This little rite was a personal favourite. It was designed to 'clear the air' of an area after some sort of conflict. It was designed to heal areas where there had been some murder, violence or even warfare. However there is no reason why it should not be used following domestic conflicts too.

This rite is partly done in your mind's eye and partly upon Bith. In thy acts thou should see your self as moving throughout the perimeters of the area of discord even though you might only be walking through part of it.

Prepare the space in the Ancient manner and then stand in the centre of thy circle and say:

In this place there was discord
where men hurt men
It has left its mark on every
Tree, Stone and Creature.
They sing a song of discord
And that createth greater sadness.

Stand in the position of Power and say:

I who am half man and half tree
I who have my feet on the ground and can touch the sky.
I who am a creature of flaming water
I who am in a place that is no-where and everywhere.
Call upon the powers of the Ather into this place to heal
  it.

(Sing the note of the Ather. Visualise white light coming from thy hand and filling the area.)

I who am half man and half tree
I who have my feet on the ground and can touch the sky.
I who am a creature of flaming water
I who am in a place that is no-where and everywhere,
call upon the powers of the Mather into this place to
heal it.

(Sing the note of the Mather. Visualise red light coming from thy hand and filling the area)

I who am half man and half tree
I who have my feet on the ground and can touch the sky.
I who am a creature of flaming water
I who am in a place that is no-where and everywhere,

Call upon the powers of the Amhran into this place to heal it.

(Sing the note of the Mather. Visualise rose light coming from thy hand and filling the area. You must see the rose light in everything possible in the area and singing back the perfected note).

When this is done Say:

Verily that the blessing of the Amhran hath descended upon this place
Let it be a place of peace
Let it be a place of inspiration
Let it be free from discord
From now until the Amhran finishes the Singing.

Second-Grade Rite

This rite was conducted in a cave, in a house, or, as in one case I know of, in a barrow. It is important to keep things as dark as possible so that when the lanterns are opened they have a tremendous impact on the candidate. To that end we used to place the hooded lanterns in cabinets with a small hole drilled in the top.

The place where we mostly met was a cave where you had to crawl to get in and space inside was at a premium. However the sound we got when we sang the Notes in that place was phenomenal. The thunder sheet was a piece of sheet metal that when shook sounded like thunder. This had an impressive effect in a cave or barrow but less so in a house. In the later days of the rite we used to ignite photographic flash powder when the thunder crashed so that the skull was illuminated for a second. It was very effective, but it did tend to leave us all a bit blind for a minute.

This rite enables the Druid to access Tir Andoman for the first time, although they would have touched on its borders during their communions with Nature in Bith. This was the test of whether someone was ready for the

Second Degree when their mentor noted that they were starting to stray into the Tir Andoman.

During this rite they will be introduced to the Ancestors, the Faery, the Gods and Goddesses and finally the Emerald Heart of the World. They will also be shown the Tir Andoman adaptations of the four elements, which have their roots in this place. I have noted that some of these elements, and indeed the Emerald Heart itself, have correlations with the Hallows of the Grail legends. They have a different meaning here but I often wondered who inspired whom. There is a tendency among modern pagan authors to say that the Grail legends were shadows of the Druidic mysteries as told by the bards of the 12th century. I doubt that very much as the thing that always struck me about those legends was that they emphasised Christianity and its rites rather than the Druids and theirs.

Rulers of the cave.

All Druids, including Rulers of the Cave should wear Ubhs and carry their staffs.
Merlin: Pendragon bracelets, Staff of Oak, a human skull, hooded lamp and thunder sheet.
White Pendragon: White Pendragon staff, a spear, hooded lamp.
Red Pendragon: Red Pendragon staff, a cauldron, hooded lamp
Amhran : With seven stringed harp, mirror of Bronze, hooded lamp, and cloak.
2nd Cucullati sword and cloak
3rd Cucullati sword and cloak

The candidates should be given a bowl of milk to drink while they wait and should be placed out of earshot of the rite. Ideally they should be kept in as much light as possible. They should wear their druid's egg and have their personal staff.

The temple should be establised as the first degree, save only there should be no grave, or cauldron placed. The need-fire should be built as before out of seven sacred woods. Beside the throne of the Merlin should be placed a pediment upon which is placed the skull. The officers could also have stands for their hooded lanterns.

The Setting Aside

Amhran walks to the Merlin who hands him a dagger of Bronze. Amhran then walks behind him and in a clockwise circle that encloses the whole rite (excluding the candidate) thrice. As this is done he says:-

> *I set aside this place in Bith.*
> *I set aside this place in the Tir Andoman.*
> *In this Kingdom Time is Not*
> *In this Kingdom Light and Darkness are Not*
> *In this Kingdom All things are Oinacos*
> *I seal this place with the Ring-Pass-Not of Bronze*
> *I seal this place in the Name of the Mather*
> *I seal this place in the Name of the Ather.*
> *I seal this place in the Name of the Song which binds.*

Amhran gives the Knife of Bronze to the Merlin and goes before the Altar. He plays a scale on the Harp.

Merlin: (striking staff): *The riddle is born. I am one and alone, yet I Create Three. Who am I?*

White Pendragon: *Light.*

Red Pendragon: *Dark.*

Amhran: *Thou art the circle of fire. Thou art the Night's dark sky pricked with the Light of the Stars.*

Merlin: *How did I create?*

White Pendragon: *With the White Pendragon of Fire.*

Red Pendragon: *With the Red Pendragon of Water.*

Amhran: *Taking both Pendragons entwined in thy arms you created the first Breath and the first Stone.*

Merlin raises arms in the Position of Creation and then crashes bracelets together and then sings:

OOOOOOOOOOOOOOOOOOOOOOOOOOOOOO
UUUUUUUUUUUUUUUUUUUUUUUUUUUUUU
EEEEEEEEEEEEEEEEEEEEEEEEEEEEEEEE

As he sings OOOOOOOO so does the White Pendragon sing OOOOOOOO. When He sings UUUUUUUUUU likewise does the Red Pendragon sing UUUUUUUUUUUUUUUUUU and when EEEEEEEEEEEEE Amhran sings EEEEEEEEEEEEEE.

Merlin: *Why doth I create?*

White Pendragon: *For it is thine own self*

Red Pendragon: *To Name thyself*

Amhran: *To hold a perfect image of thyself, to know who thou art.*

Merlin: *Show me my image*

Amhran plays seven notes.
 Then when he is finished the holds up his mirror and says:-

Amhran: *Behold the Song and the Singer.*

All take their staffs and knock three times three on the ground. The Amhran plays the scale of seven notes.

The Rite of Tir Andoman

Merlin: *Caste of the Druid Order of Pendragon, hear the word of the Merlin. A child student of our Order hath strayed too far into Tir Andoman in his studies into Nature and has realised the world beyond.*

Amhran: *Amhran is in his breast his path will take him to the Emerald Heart of the Earth if he comes not to harm on the way.*

Merlin: *Therefore it is our will that his Ubh be opened to the powers of the Cucullati that he may be protected* *in his quest.*

Allow him to open the gate to Tir Andoman and bring him forth.

Amhran leaves and brings the candidate and instructs him on how to open the gate in the following manner.

Amhran: *Mealog, in thy quest, thou hast fumbled at the lock of the door to brightness and death. This is a door to which thou art not permitted lest thee be blinded or driven from the world of Bith. Doest thou understand?*

Mealog nods

Be that as it may, the Merlin hath decided that which thou hast opened a crack shall be opened unto to you, that you may learn what is on the other side. However, he has sent me and mine as a guide unto you. I am the first of the beings known as the Cucullati and I speak for my people.

In thy first initiation thou walkest through a small part of this kingdom to make thine oath and the rule thou were taught on that occasion no longer standeth still namely:

In that land look neither left nor right,
Neither up nor down.
Take no food nor water.
Talk to none but she who would answer thy purpose.
Now thou must look, speak, hear and understand, touch and taste thou must not least they will remaineth here forever.

You enter the Tir Andoman through the hollow hills, through a portal covered with blood and milk. Take thy cauldron of sacrifice and pour the blood on the right side of this portal and the milk on the left.

Mealog does so

Draw thy Ogham name between the portal and sing the name of the Ather, the name of the Mather and the name of the Amhran.

Mealog does so.

> *Thus, by the name of the three that are one, the Portal to Tir Andoman is open unto thee, enter to thy reward or doom.*

The Mealog enters the portal with the Amhran behind him. As he enters the Merlin uses the thunder sheet and lights up the candle before the skull.

Red Pendragon: *Why comest thou unto the land of the dead, why comest thou to Tir Naharbh. Thy head is mine!*

The two Cucullati draw their swords and place them across the candidate's throat.

Amhran: *One who cometh into Tir Naharbh with the blessing of the Merlin of the Druidic Order of the Pendragon. Cucullati thou art his kin for now and ever more, in the name of the Amhran.*

The Cucullati stand on either side of the Mealog. The light before the skull is snuffed out. The Red Pendragon opens the lantern so that it casts light across her face.

Red Pendragon: *I am the spirit of all women. I have been a mother, a queen, a lover, and a warrior.*

Amhran: *Thou art a woman no longer. Thou art a shadow of a being long departed, a memory kept alive by the Emerald Heart of the Earth which I seek.*

The White Pendragon opens the lantern so that it casts light across his face.

White Pendragon: *I am the spirit of all men. I have been a father, a king, a lover, and a warrior.*

Amhran: *Thou art a man no longer. Thou art a shadow of a being long departed, a memory kept alive by the Emerald Heart of the Earth which I seek.*

The two Pendragons shut off their lights

The Merlin lights the candle in front of the skull and says:

Merlin: *Hast thou no respect for thine ancestors Dweller in Bith? Are they not what you were and what you will be?*

Amhran: *My true self rises with the Amhran unto the Stone of Oinacos*

Merlin: *Well met Dweller in Bith. However know this that all human knowledge is to be found in Tir Naharbh would thou wish to have this knowledge?*

Amhran: *I would.*

Merlin then steps forward into the triangle of the Mather.

Red and White Pendragons light their lanterns and the Mealog, the Cucullati and the Amhran step forward.

Merlin raises arms in the Position of Creation and then crashes bracelets together and then sings:

OOOOOOOOOOOOOOOOOOOOOOOOOOOOOO
UUUUUUUUUUUUUUUUUUUUUUUUUUUUUU
EEEEEEEEEEEEEEEEEEEEEEEEEEEEEEEE

As he sings OOOOOOOO so does the White Pendragon sing OOOOOOOO. When he sings UUUUUUUUUU likewise does the Red Pendragon sing UUUUUUUUUUUUUUUUUU and when EEEEEEEEEEEEE Amhran sings EEEEEEEEEEEEEE.

Red Pendragon advances and gives the candidate a sword saying:

Red Pendragon: *I arm thee with wisdom in the name of the Mather.*

White Pendragon advances and gives the candidate a spear saying:

White Pendragon: *I arm thee with power in the name of the Ather.*

Amhran: *Drink thee from the cauldron of remembrance so that the Spirits of the ancestors might teach thee.*

Mealog does so.

Merlin rises and takes the skull and places it on top of the candidate's head.

Merlin: *With this head, which was sacrificed for this purpose, I give thee the power of the King (or Queen) of the Dead.*

pause

> *With these four powers, the sword, the spear, the head and the cauldron thou hast found the root of the elemental powers. In using them in balance thou shalt enter the next kingdom of Tir Andoman that of the Gods and Goddesses. Place the elements in the position of balance.*

The Mealog, with the help of the Merlin and Cucullati, builds a square out of the implements, with him standing in the middle. They put the head in the East, the Cauldron in the West, the Sword in the North and the Spear in the South. When this is done all lights should be extinguished.

Red Pendragon: *The Journey continues into the depths of Tir Andoman.*

White Pendragon: *All about are the cries of the dead.*

Red Pendragon: *Some of joy.*

White Pendragon: *Some of pain.*

Red Pendragon: *Back, back and further back*

White Pendragon: *To the Dawn of humanity.*

Merlin: *When the first man gave part of himself to be his God.*

The thunder sheet is rolled again[8] and the White Pendragon reveals his light and holds his hammer.

---

[8] It was here we used our photograph flash powder.

White Pendragon: *I am the King of the Gods. Walk in fear before my flashing lightning. I give wisdom to those who would need it but destroy those who fail me. Worship me mortal and I shall give you wisdom and power.*

Amhran: *Thou art a shadow of the true Ather, a memory kept alive by the Emerald Heart of the Earth which I seek. Men created you, yet you demand of me your worship? Nay, creature of the Amhran and of discord, I am a creature of the Song and the Spark and worship none but these.*

Red Pendragon reveals her light and holds her cauldron.

Red Pendragon: *I am the Queen of the Gods. Walk in fear before my warbands of death. I give birth and death unto the world and destroy those who fail me. Worship me mortal and I shall give thee a life of glory.*

Amhran: *Thou art a shadow of the true Mather, a memory kept alive by the Emerald Heart of the Earth which I seek. Men created you yet you demand of me your worship? Nay creature of the Amhran and of discord, I am a creature of the Song and the Spark and worship none but these.*

Merlin: *Who is this that would stand against the Gods even unto his death by their hands?*

Amhran: *My true self rises with the Amhran unto the Stone of Oinacos. I who am searching for unity have no need for shattered fragments of human fears.*

Merlin: *Well met, Dweller in Bith. However, in each God there is a portion of many men's power, which they have gifted to another being. In the Kingdoms of the Gods and Goddesses this divine Wisdom and Power can be obtained. Would thou bring back the birthright of other men?*

Amhran: *I would.*

Merlin: *Then take thou the gift of the Gods.*

White Pendragon pours milk on the ground before the candidate. Red Pendragon pours wine on the ground before the candidate. Merlin comes forward and holds a crown of Mistletoe over the candidate.

Merlin: *With this Crown of Sacrifice, I give thee the power of the King (or Queen) of the Gods.*

Merlin places the crown on the Mealog's head. Returns to his place and all lights are extinguished.

Red Pendragon: *The Journey continues into the depths of Tir Andoman.*

White Pendragon: *Through the Kingdom of the Gods.*

Red Pendragon: *Some of joy*

White Pendragon: *Some of dread.*

Red Pendragon: *Back, back and further back*

White Pendragon: *To the Dawn of humanity.*

Amhran: *When the Amhran placed himself in the heart of creation to give it life.*

Merlin unveils a single lamp.

Red Pendragon: *He placed himself in the centre of a green crystal at the centre of the Earth.*

White Pendragon: *And the energy radiated throughout creation giving life to all.*

Merlin: *Yet if you searcheth upon the earth thou wilt not find its Emerald Heart.*

Red Pendragon: *If you searched in the depths of Tir Andoman you would not find it.*

White Pendragon: *If you searched in the depths of Mag Mor you would not find it.*

Amhran: *Yet it is in all these places but especially in Tir Andoman where it provideth sustenance to the Gods and the Ancestors.*

Merlin: *But what should the candidate look for?*

Amhran: *The Emerald Heart of the World is many shapes and creatures. It is the Song of Power that uniteth all beings seen and unseen. It is found everywhere and no where. Ever fixed it cannot be volatile Ever volatile it cannot be fixed. That which does not change is not the Emerald Stone. Yet all things change. The Stone is found by vision and aspiration And when found you will be reborn As the Amhran.*

Merlin: *Let us call upon the Amhran to grant this candidate a healing vision so that he may see, feel, and hear the Emerald Heart of the World.*

Red and White Pendragon step forward and form a triangle arch above the Candidate. The Cacullati mirror them. The Amhran steps back to form a triangle with the other Cacullati. When this is done the Merlin veils the white light and prepares the Green lamp, but does not reveal it.

Merlin: *Let us then ask the Amhran for his blessing.*

Merlin raises arms in the Position of Creation and then crashes bracelets together and then sings:

*OOOOOOOOOOOOOOOOOOOOOOOOOOOOOOOO
UUUUUUUUUUUUUUUUUUUUUUUUUUUUUU
EEEEEEEEEEEEEEEEEEEEEEEEEEEEEEEEE*

As he sings OOOOOOOO so does the White Pendragon sing OOOOOOOO. When he sings UUUUUUUUUUU likewise does the Red Pendragon sing UUUUUUUUUUUUUUUUU and when EEEEEEEEEEEEE Amhran sings EEEEEEEEEEEEEE.

Merlin reveals the Green lantern and carries it towards the candidate slowly.

Merlin: *The Emerald Light at the Centre of the Earth approacheth.*
The light of thy very being cometh.
It healeth
It strengthens
It inspires
Now
And forever more.

He holds it over the Mealog's breast.

In the name of the Amhran I seal this vision within thy heart. A living vision that will heal and empower thee in thy journeys in Bith and Tir Andoman.

OOOOOOOOOOOOOOOOOOOOOOOOOOOOOO
UUUUUUUUUUUUUUUUUUUUUUUUUUUUUU
EEEEEEEEEEEEEEEEEEEEEEEEEEEEEEEE

As he sings OOOOOOOO so does the White Pendragon sing OOOOOOOO. When he sings UUUUUUUUUUU likewise does the Red Pendragon sing UUUUUUUUUUUUUUUUUU and when EEEEEEEEEEEEEEEE Amhran sings EEEEEEEEEEEEEE.

When this is done he says:

Ovate thy wanderings have carried thee into Tir Andoman. Now with the blessing and protection of this Order though mayest continue. Depart Tir Andoman for now to carry on thy quest at a later time.

The Amhran escorts new Ovate from the cave and returns for the closure.

The Closure

Merlin (striking staff and stands in the position of Power):

I am half man and half tree, who walks betwixt worlds whose feet touch the earth and whose hands reach heaven. Within my breast is the seed of the Oinacos. In its name I make the three Worlds one again.

[White Pendragon sings the AAAAAAAAAAAAAAAA. Red Pendragon sings the OOOOOOOOOOOOOOOOO. Amhran sings the UUUUUUUUUUUUUUUUUU. This is done simultaneously].

Melin: *The riddle is answered the rite is done, the worlds are aligned. Let us depart unto our groves in peace.*

Of the Rulers of the Cave

General

The Rulers of the Cave in the Second Grade rite represent the forces at play in Tir Andoman. The Merlin is the spark of the Oinacos, the Red Pendragon is the Mather, the White Pendragon is the Ather and Amhran is represented by the officer with that name and by the Candidate. This time the Amhran is the chief of a group of three other rulers called the Cacullati.

Merlin

Dressed as in the first grade only on his brow, in red paint or wine this time, should be a moon crescent, which haveth a direct correspondence with the action of the Oinacos in Tir Andoman. He has a staff of Hazel and a bronze knife in his belt upon which is written in Ogham AOU in a triangle as before. He also has the

---

[9] The Skull used in the Order was real and had an injury to the top of the head. The Merlin said that it belonged to a former member of the Order who before going off to fight for the Royalists as a foot soldier in the English Civil War said that if he were killed he hoped that it would be enough of a sacrifice to warrant his skull being used in the Order. He was apparently killed when his unit fled and while he stood his ground he was struck in the head. The army scattered and almost senseless in the aftermath of the battle he struggled home and died. The story did not say how the Order collected the head.

human skull which is placed on a pedestal before a short candle on his left side. When holding the skull, he is representing the divine force that is responsible for the dead[9]. This force is a combination of the Song and the Spark and decides when part of human life is over and makes the transition possible. He also carries a lantern that showeth green light, which represents the Emerald Heart of the World.

Red Pendragon

Is dressed as in the first grade. However this time she has a sword with which she arms the candidate for his future journey.

White Pendragon

Likewise is dressed as in the first grade. This time he carries a spear with which he arms the candidate.

Amhran

Is dressed in a hooded cloak as part of his office as the lead Cucullati. On his brow in red paint or wine should be drawn the letter U in Ogham. He does not carry his harp in this grade but still carries his mirror.

2nd and 3rd Cacullati

These are hooded and cloaked so that their faces are not showing. They carry iron swords to protect the candidate and prevent trespassers from entering the rites when the cave is moved to Tir Andoman.

Of the Cacullati

The mysterious figures of the Cacullati appear in many different inscriptions found throughout the British Isles, particularly during the Roman period. However archaeologists and historians are at a loss to explain their function. There are always three and two carry swords. They are sometimes seen in the presence of a Goddess who holds an egg. They have been variously described as guardians of the Goddess.

However, symbols that are meaningless to modern historians, have considerable import when looked at from the perspective of this Order.

Firstly such pictures are shadows of ceremonies whose meaning was lost on the general public. However when Druids entered the priesthoods of the various Roman Gods and Goddesses it was inevitable that some of our teaching should filter into their respective cults, admittedly in a veiled manner. According to Order papers worshippers were told that such creatures would protect them in the after life and not do them any good in this one. This prevented people worshipping them to request help in Bith and thus enabled them to stay in Tir Andoman, never actually becoming Gods.

In actual fact, however, the Cacullati were guardian figures in Tir Andoman for Druids. Two were mute and their function was simply to protect and the other had the role of diplomat between us and the denizens of that world. Like Gods and Goddesses men created them, but in this case it was the members of the Druid Order. Many centuries ago they created forms in their minds and ensouled them with elements of their own song - just like profane men did with their Gods. They placed in them their ability to protect and communicate and effectively created Gods and Goddesses who could move amongst Tir Andoman. They did not need to be worshipped, as they did not need to ever leave the Tir Andoman. Likewise because members of this Order have never forgotten them, they have not disappeared into the depths of Tir Andoman where they cannot be found. Instead they wait by the threshold of any portal opened by a Druid. They also stand guard in any rite which calls upon all members and can been seen by those with Sight as standing in the West.

The historical representations of the Cucullati are sometimes shown as approaching a Mother Goddess. This is a shadow illusion to the Mather who is depicted as the Goddess of the Temple where the Druid is officiating. She is shown holding an egg (sometimes three) as a symbol to the profane (as of being birth in the Tir Andoman). The Order teaches that these are flaming Ubh of a Druid as he passes through Tir Andoman in his search for the Emerald Heart in the Centre of the Earth. The Mather rules Tir Andoman and the Druid is in her hands with the assistance of the Cacullati.

In our ritual, the lead Cacullati is represented by the Amhran, because he is the one who speaks on behalf of the candidate. In thy journeys in Tir Andoman this One who Speaks will act as your guide and ambassador between thyself and the Tir Andoman creatures. Simply tell him what you want to do and say and he will make sure that you don't come to harm. The other Cucullati provide a force that in Tir Andoman appears physical if a being would attempt to attack you.

There are several types of creatures that could do you harm. There are the more discordant Gods or ancestors who might see you as a threat or who, in the case of Gods, might be gravely insulted that you will not worship them. Then there are the Faery who are the most likely to attack you.

The presence of the Cucullati will create respect and if that is not enough then they are capable of doing harm. The power of the Right Handed Cucullati comes from the White Pendragon and the Left Handed one comes from the Red. They draw power from the Green Emerald at the Heart of the Earth and have an additional current to the Pendragons, which effectively gives them unlimited power. The Cucullati Who Speaks draws his powers from both and is closely tuned to the note of the Amhran.

Address to the candidate of the Second Grade

This grade deals with the greatest of fears, that of mortality and death. A Druid does not fear such things because he believes that the essential part of him will be reborn and has visited the lands of the dead and its processes hold nothing new. This rite will guide encounters in Tir Andoman and opens part of your Ubh so that you can experience and control these states. It has two effects, one is in the Mind and the other is as a result of the magical manipulation of the Ubh.

In your studies you have learnt that the Ubh has different parts. Now the first degree deals with the Ubh of fire, which is attributed to the Amhran[10]. This degree manipulates the Ubhmather that is

---

[10] They are reflected and reversed. The Amhran is everywhere, however when the universal force of the Ather operates on the body it creates a similar structure that is seen in the Universe, but uses the Amhran to do it.

attributed to the Mather. This is the membrane and 'white', which exists between the Ubh of fire and the Ubhather. Like the rest of the substance of the Ubhmather this membrane can be tuned so that it opens to certain forces.

In this ritual the Rulers of the Cave work their magic to impress on your Ubhmather certain tokens. When these are activated in the course of your Other World journeys you will find that your Inner Senses are clearer and that your powers are greater.

The first thing you are told is that you have attained this grade by accident that you have stumbled across something dangerous that you shouldn't have. This may have come as some surprise to you however there will have been moments when you have been doing your communing work where you have taken the element a fraction deeper than normal. At this point you would have opened the doors to Tir Andoman a crack to see that part of nature's roots.

The fact that you have been able to do this is a sign that you will soon be straying into that realm unguarded and unprotected, but it also means that you have started to outgrow the lessons of the first degree. But forget not thy studies in this area, however alluring Tir Andoman appeareth. You will never cease looking for the Song in Nature, that is one of the central tenets of Druidry.

Next you are shown, independently of any rite how to enter Tir Andoman (these missives give another method that you may use for your personal work). This is because you are expected to enter these realms by yourself without assistance from now on.

When you enter you encounter the creatures of the Pendragon, the Cucullati. In the first instance they see you as a threat to the rite which is being performed, because they stand as guardians of the Order. When you are given permission to pass they stand to your right and left hand and will protect you for the rest of your life. The Amhran plays the role of the Cacullati Who Speaks. This particular Cucullati is a guide for thee until thou has reached a standard of Wisdom where you can speak for thine own self.

When the Amhran is building the yolk around the Spark in the centre of the person it is using the principle of concentrated seeding expressed by the Ather.

However this encounter is the first you have with the Dread Lord of the Death who is represented by the skull. You are challenged by the Ancestors and you reject their pleas for attention. You are advised that they have much to teach you if you are careful. You agree to accept their gifts that are the primal symbols of the elements that they guard. These are the Sword of Earth, the Spear of Fire, the Head of Air and the Cauldron of Water. These are the elements that you were starting to discover the meaning of when you stumbled into Tir Andoman.

The symbols of these primal elements are then fused into your Ubhmather in a balanced way so that you can use them in thy journey. You are crowned as the King (or Queen) of the Dead. This is a token in thy Ubh, which means that thou can be recognised by the beings of the Tir Naharbh as one in authority. In their dealings with thee they are not likely not to see beyond this token unless they are highly developed beings, in which case they are likely to recognise the token as the respected authority of the Order.

After this you come to the part of Tir Andoman that is ruled by the Gods and Goddesses. Again you correctly dismissed them, but were told that they had much power they could give you if you are careful.

You agree to accept their gifts, which are represented by the sacrifice to thee of Milk and Wine (blood). This is a sign that the Gods and Goddesses are swearing thee fealty. Because this act has been done in a rite in the presence of others and divinely invoked formulas it makes it more difficult for Creatures of the Song to stand against this urge to assist thee in thy journeys.

Thou art given a crown of mistletoe to indicate thy powers over the Gods and Goddesses. But when this Crown is placed upon you this symbol of the sacrifice of the Amhran is fused into the Ubhmather. It indicates that by being crowned by the Amhran thou art the same status as the Gods. This token is recognised by the Gods and Goddesses, even if they will attempt to convince thee of thy mortality.

Next there comes the vision of the Emerald Heart of the World that is the most physical representation of the Amhran. On the surface it appears that you are presented with a vision of the stone so that in your quest it will be easier to find, however the rite achieves much more than this. In sealing the vision into your Ubh you are provided with a line between the Stone and thy heart. This act, while not as powerful as beholding the Emerald Heart itself, provides the Druid with many of its gifts.

Once again, you are escorted from the Temple and are not permitted to see the closing ceremony. The reason for this is similar. Initiation rites within the Order do not to take thee deeper into a fraternity, it is designed to assist thee over thresholds in thy development, once these are overcome thou journeyest upon thy own knowledge. Notwithstanding this statement, the Order is a place of fraternal nourishment but only in its regular rites and festivals. But an initiation is a more personal rite and is seen as something separate from the rest of our work.

The work of this Grade is to visit the Tir Andoman often and learn from its inhabitants. However this does not mean the finishing of thy work in Bith. This work never finishes until thy function within the Song is completed. Just as thou must continue thy work looking for the Song in Nature, now you must also seek for it in Tir Andoman in the form of the Emerald Heart of the World.

Chapter Four

The Third Grade – Druid

The Druid Degree was the culmination of the work of the Order and was performed only after the Ovate had experienced some sort of vision of the Emerald Heart of the World in Tir Andoman. Although there was less core grade material for a Druid the actual work, along with the continuance of their work in Bith and Tir Andoman took a lifetime. Firstly there was the mastery of the Notes of the Wanderers, which in itself took a long time, and then there was the integration of the Rulers of the Grove and finally the passing through and replacement of the Merlin. These are all depicted in the Druid ritual and really need no explanation, except to say that once a person had truly become what is represented in this grade they were certainly not quite human! I have only seen four people in my time who had truly attained it, two of them were Merlin of the Order, one had the role of the Amhran in the Order for nearly 20 years and the other played the Mather or Red Pendragon. None of these people felt able to step in the shoes of the last Merlin as the other two felt they were too old. I am sure that a Group starting up today would have the assistance from Tir Andoman that they need, but we felt that as people who had gone a long way down a path we could not now say that the rules had changed. For what it is worth I believe that now, after all these years, I have come close to touching the hem of the Amhran but it will take another couple of lifetimes before I can confidently hold a mirror to the One Thing.

Of Mag Mor

Mag Mor is the land of the Ather and is the final part of the three fold creation of the world. It is like unto Tir Andoman as Tir Andoman is to Bith. [*It is another dimension at right angles to it.* C.R.] Confuse it not with the skies, although these have a direct correlation with Mag Mor. The physical sky as we see it is a shadow of the life in the realm of the Ather and when we watch the clouds it showeth a dim reflection of what is going on in that kingdom.

Thus we attend to the skies so that some inkling of what will befall humanity will become clear. Storms and great winds can be portents of change, particularly if they are out of season.

In the skies beyond the fire that surrounds the Earth are the physical expressions of the Wanderers whose acts are described in the Art of Astrology. At the centre is the Sun about which all notes including the Earth moveth. Each with their special note they make great music in the Universe and that music createth the web of destiny from which we are threads.

Yet know this that when thou looketh into the heavens thou seeth only a shadow of Mag Mor, or rather we are a shadow for it. [*If Tir Andoman is at 90 degrees to Bith, then Mag Mor is at 180 which would put it as a direct reflection to the material world. The order taught that you could approach the wanderers by using meditation and rites connected with the Book of the Amhran. However it also said that this would only give you a reflection of the truth. This is because such methods only work with the fluid matter of Tir Andoman. To really understand the Note of the planet you would have to journey to Mag Mor and experience it directly. This is only possible through your experience with the Emerald Heart of the World. Essentially you use this to enter the land of Mag Mor and this is extremely hard to do, but by using the Book it becomes easier.* C.R.]

Much is lost through the reflection and the only way to truly approach the notes of the planets is by journeying first through Tir Andoman and entering into Mag Mor through thy vision of the Emerald Heart of the World.

Then thou wilt seeth the power of the Ather and be able to approach each and every note in a truth rather than by reflection.

Mag Mor is built of fire and the Notes of the Wanderers hang like coloured balls of vibration. At the heart of the Kingdom is the Sun and closest to it is Teachdaire (Mercury) which acts as a messenger between the Ather and the rest of creation.

Next cometh Baidh (Venus) who bringeth forth love into creation, for through love are all things bought together in the Amhran.

Then there is Mairt (Mars) who moveth all things unto action and reaction.

Then there is Luan (Moon) through which door the nurturing powers of the Mather enter into creation.

Then there is Domhnall (Jupiter) who ruleth and expandeth the development of creation.

And finally there is Sathurn (Saturn) who causes all limitations and death.

When thou entereth Mag Mor thou shalt first encounter the forces of Sathurn who will attempt to turn thee away. For it is their role to keep you in creation. From them thou shalt learn the secrets of death so that you mayest be reborn in Mag Mor. They are of fearful countenance but fear them not, for they are creatures of the Amhran and are thy cousins.

Next thou shall meeteth the expansive forces of Domhnall. All powers of the universe are at his disposal and he will test thee by offering them unto you. If you follow his way, fame and fortune will be thine, but you will become lost in creation. Instead he should teach you how to rule as a God thine own domain and destiny.

Next thou should meeteth Luan who shall attempt to confuse thee with images and illusion. The act of nurturing creation is likened unto a mother who wishes her prodigy to leave not. She will stand against ye. But her note also reveals all the memories of Creation and calms the seas.

Mairt moves all things and is the life force of creation. Yet he shall also do thee violence or cause you to do violence unto others. He would move thee beyond thy thread of destiny into unfamiliar lands where thou would recant thy rashness. Yet he will teach thee how to use your energy wisely, creatively and enable you to press on towards thy goal.

In meeting Baidh thou art cleaved unto the love force of the Universe and merge unto it. Yet there is also the danger of sensuality overwhelming thee as thou hear this note you shall see the beauty of the Song, but shall rejoice in your reflection in it.

In meeting Teachdaire you become aware of the true poem or song of the Universe and communicate it between the different layers of the Universe. There is a danger, so close to the Amhran itself, that you shall mistake Teachdaire for the Song. For as you communicate its message so ye shall be consumed by it for mastery of this note has made thee much more of a God or Goddess for you are the voice of the Amhran on Earth.

Grian is the Amhran made manifest in Creation. It is the highest state that any human may be. As such naught may be spoken for it is beyond all poetry and no image may contain it.

Thus when all these notes are sung in Mag Mor are all things created of fire. In this state the Human corresponds to the living image of the Mather and in doing so draws upon his experience in Bith and Tir Andoman and becomes the very embodiment of the Amhran.

But even then the work of the Druid remains undone for it is the work of creation to stand before the Oinacos and hold up the mirror of their lives and say:-

"This part of creation is who you are." This act causes the created to merge into the Oinacos and to become truly itself.

The names of the Wanderers (Allabanrind)

These are:
Mairt,   Mars
Baidh,   Venus
Grian,   Sun
Luan,   Moon

Domhnall,	Jupiter
Sathurn,	Saturn
Teachdaire,	Mercury

Of the seals of the Zodiac

Before the introduction of Ogham the Druids used a system of representing the Wanderers, the Zodiacal powers, the Ather, the Mather and Amhran with seals. After the introduction of Ogham they were only used by the Pendragon caste who had their own from time immemorial. They were sometimes drawn with or without the Ogham and there was considerable difference between each Druid on what the final arrangement should be. All the order required was that a Druid demonstrate that his or her arrangement generated the right Note.

The rules are the following: the Oinacos was represented by a point, the Ather by a line, the Mather by a Triangle and Amhran by a circle or curve. A spiral moving inwards and outwards depicted the movement of Amhran throughout creation. Energy was shown as a jagged line or a lightning flash to represent the Ather in motion. A Triangle turns an energy into a seed so that it may grow on all levels.

These examples of the images were used to represent the seals of the Zodiac. When drawn on an object they shall partake of the virtues of the Note from which the signs are created.

The Third Grade - Druid

The Archer   The Goat

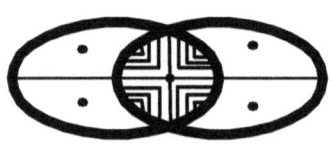

Water Carrier   Fishes

Of the seals of the Wanderers.

These are the seals of the Wanderers. When drawn on an object they shall partake of the virtues of the Note from which the Wanderer is created. Note that the Sun and the Moon do partake of the virtues of the Ather and the Mather respectively.

Teachdaire

The book of the Amhran

Introduction

This is the Book of the Amhran. It was originally written on ten tablets of Stone that were placed in the College of Pendragon upon the Isle of Mona. After his initiation the Druid was lead to a stone circle and was allowed to copy the pages from this ancient book on the earth below his feet until he could remember each page. Before the Romans came the Pendragon removed the stones to Tara, but bought them back after they had gone. They were smashed to prevent them falling into the hands of the Christians, as some Druids had converted to that religion and would have had them away.

But it was not the magic of these stones that should have been feared but rather the words that were placed upon them. They were of no language of men, but rather the sounds of the Amhran describing every note of creation. Mastery of a page gave mastery of the note and the very symbols themselves contain powerful magical words. Using this book enables the Druid to create songs for each being in Creation and bring them harm or happiness.

Of the letters of the book – The Amhran Alphabet

Each letter does not use the Ogham alphabet, which it predates by countless generations. It uses the principles of sounds of the note and their attribution to the Ather, Mather and Amhran. As an alphabet it is impractical because each letter would take too long to draw, however as a sacred way of creating the sounds of creation it is extremely potent. Although the actual notes are the same the Alphabet generates an collection of sounds different from that which was taught in the earlier grades.

This is because this alphabet was considered so secret that only those who had seen the Emerald Heart of the World were permitted access to it. It was also not used even in the First or Second

Grade initiation rites for fear that it might accidentally open an inappropriate page of the book of the Amhran or that it might be copied by those unable to handle its powers.

Pronunciation

Each letter was attributed to either the Ather, Mather or Amhran. An Ather letter was pronounced by vibrating against the back of the mouth to give a jagged nasal sound and was lower. If anyone has heard Tibetan monks chanting their mantras they would have an idea of what these notes sounded like.

A Mather letter was sung higher than the mid range through a mouth shaped like an 'O' *[I was always reminded of the pictures of choir boys when I saw Druids singing Mather letters. The Amhran sound was with the mouth wide open. The Oinacos sound was never pronounced but was instead a space between letters. C.R.]*

Of the letters of the book — The Amhran Alphabet

Letter	Shape	Three Fold Classification	Planetary Zodiacal
A	⊚	Amhran	Amhran
E	○	Amhran	Mercury
I	⊕	Mather	Venus

O	✛	Ather	Sun
U	☾	Mather	Moon
B	⚡	Ather	Mars
h	⛰	Ather	Jupiter
M	WM	Ather	Saturn
N	∧∨	Ather	Lion
F	∫	Mather	Scorpion
R	e	Mather	Bull
S	♋	Amhran	Man
C	◊	Mather	Fishes

z	◠	Amhran	Twins
q	△	Mather	Crab
T	↑	Ather	Archer
G	▽	Mather	Virgin
Ng	⌒	Amhran	Scales
L	M	Ather	Ram
O	XX	Mather	Goat

Letter	Musical Note
A	C
E	E
I	F
O	C
U	D
B	G
H	A
M	B
N	C
F	G
R	F
S	B
C	A
Z	E
Q	D
T	A
G	E
Ng	F
L	G
D	B

Uses of the Book of Amhran

If thou was to seek for power over a particular tree thou would first divine its astrological planet; this would give thou the tablet to refer to. You would then attempt by art, intuition or journey to Tir Andoman to ascertain the shape of the creatures name upon that tablet. Drawing that sigil on the tablet giveth thou a string of letters which are the true name and notes of the tree.

Thus an Oak tree would be placed on the table of Saturn and drawn thus

L	B	T	O	M	O	T	B	L
B	T	H	N	M	N	H	T	B
T	H	N	A	M	A	N	H	T
O	N	A	O	M	O	A	N	O
M	M	M	M	M	M	M	M	M
O	N	A	O	M	O	A	N	O
T	H	N	A	M	A	N	H	T
B	T	H	N	M	N	H	T	B
L	B	T	O	M	O	T	B	L

This shape is then read from its top mostpoint following a straight line to its end. No creature shall be known by a sign which breaks. Thus in the case of the above:

M, T, T, A, A, M, H, M

Note that as in above, if a jagged line is placed upon the tablet and strays not into another square that letter is deemed repeated. Also be aware that the sign should be drawn as large as possible within the square.

Now each of these symbols, which are created in the same way as the Planetary and zodiacal seals, can be transposed into a letter and therefore a sound. In the days of the Ancient Druids the book was kept in their heads and thus when they drew a symbol in their mind they could instantaneously link it to the pages of this book. This should be the aim of every Druid.

Such sigils, if realised correctly, giveth thee power over thy subject, but thou must also seek the note of thy will. Thus if thou would give riches to a man you must first find his name under the Wanderer which was closest to the horizon of his birth. Thou should intuit his shape and place it on the appropriate page. This will give you his true note. Thus if a man's planet were Mars and his shape were

⊙	♄	N	O	A	O	N	♄	⊙
♄	N	A	T	B	T	A	N	♄
N	A	T	L	B	L	T	A	N
A	T	L	O	B	O	L	T	O
B	B	B	B	B	B	B	B	B
O	T	L	O	B	O	L	T	O
N	A	T	L	B	L	T	A	N
♄	N	A	T	B	T	A	N	♄
⊙	♄	N	O	B	O	N	♄	⊙

You would look unto the Mars tablet and find the letters
  B, A, N, B

Which would be sung using the following musical notes:
  G, C, C, G

This process will create two names of power, one for the man and the other for his purpose. One would then weave these names of power into any appropriate invocation and draw the shape when the names are sung.

Thus:

I calleth forth the powers of Domhail [Jupiter] with the song of the seal of wealth. [the note of the shape]

ᴛ	L	N	O	ƕ	O	N	L	ᴛ
L	N	B	ᴛ	ƕ	ᴛ	B	N	L
N	B	ᴛ	ᴀ	ƕ	ᴀ	ᴛ	B	N
O	ᴛ	ᴀ	O	ƕ	O	ᴀ	ᴛ	O
ƕ	ƕ	ƕ	ƕ	ƕ	ƕ	ƕ	ƕ	ƕ
O	ᴛ	ᴀ	O	ƕ	O	ᴀ	ᴛ	O
N	B	ᴛ	ᴀ	ƕ	ᴀ	ᴛ	B	N
L	N	B	ᴛ	ƕ	ᴛ	B	N	L
ᴛ	L	N	O	ƕ	O	N	L	ᴛ

I merge thee with the song of [the person's name] *and thus create a new song.* [The person's name and the note of the seal]
By this song I bind thee [the person's name] *to the powers of Domhail.*
Sing this thrice
Thrice bound Domhail thou shalt have thee riches.

Likewise if thou wishest to create thine own protection seals or other magics thou would either draw them in the air or place them upon talismans.

From this thou shalt see that any magical rite should be easily performed, but the labour of the Druid should not be simply for this. The process of mastery of the note on each page is far more profound than profane.

If the signs of the Wanderer are drawn upon each table you shall have its note. This acts as a key to the portal of the planetary note itself.

Thus, in your mind's eye, you would project the square into the air in front of thee and then draw the sign upon it and thus shall create a vortex that, if thou would extrude thy Ubh of Fire into it thou shalt have a vision of that planet and learn much of its nature and effect upon the earth.

After time exploring each planet thou will meet the beings of the note that will give thee their names and seals so that thou mayest use them for magic or learning.

For every Druid they will give a different name and seal. What is so of the beings of the Wanderers is true also of the seals and shapes of every living creature thou seek to discover. This is because the note of each being is heard by you in an entirely different way from another man. These are unique keys unto the Druid that made them and should never be shown to another. Thus if thou canst not memorise all thy seals then instead locketh them up in a book so that no mortal eye should see them. For such seals are alive with the note that called them into being and if another should spy them, they will work upon his mind, which being uninitiated shall be unbalanced towards the powers of the shape and go about the world creating discord.

Note that the seals of the Moon and the Sun also refer unto the Mather and the Ather and shall lead thee to much knowledge about these sides of the One Thing.

The Table of the Amhran

ꜧ	ꜧ	ꜧ	ꜧ	ʌ	ꜧ	ꜧ	ꜧ	ꜧ
ꜧ	B	B	B	ʌ	B	B	B	ꜧ
ꜧ	B	Є	O	ʌ	O	Є	B	ꜧ
ꜧ	B	O	U	ʌ	U	O	B	ꜧ
ʌ	ʌ	ʌ	ʌ	ʌ	ʌ	ʌ	ʌ	ʌ
ⱆ	1	O	U	ʌ	U	O	1	ⱆ
ⱆ	1	Є	O	ʌ	O	Є	1	ⱆ
ⱆ	1	1	1	ʌ	1	1	1	ⱆ
ⱆ	ⱆ	ⱆ	ⱆ	ʌ	ⱆ	ⱆ	ⱆ	ⱆ

The Table Decoded

M	H	N	O	B	O	N	H	M
H	N	A	T	B	T	A	N	H
N	A	T	L	B	L	T	A	N
O	T	L	O	B	O	L	T	O
B	B	B	B	B	B	B	B	B
O	T	L	O	B	O	L	T	O
N	A	T	L	B	L	T	A	N
H	N	A	T	B	T	A	N	H
M	H	N	O	B	O	N	H	M

Mairt

The Third Grade - Druid

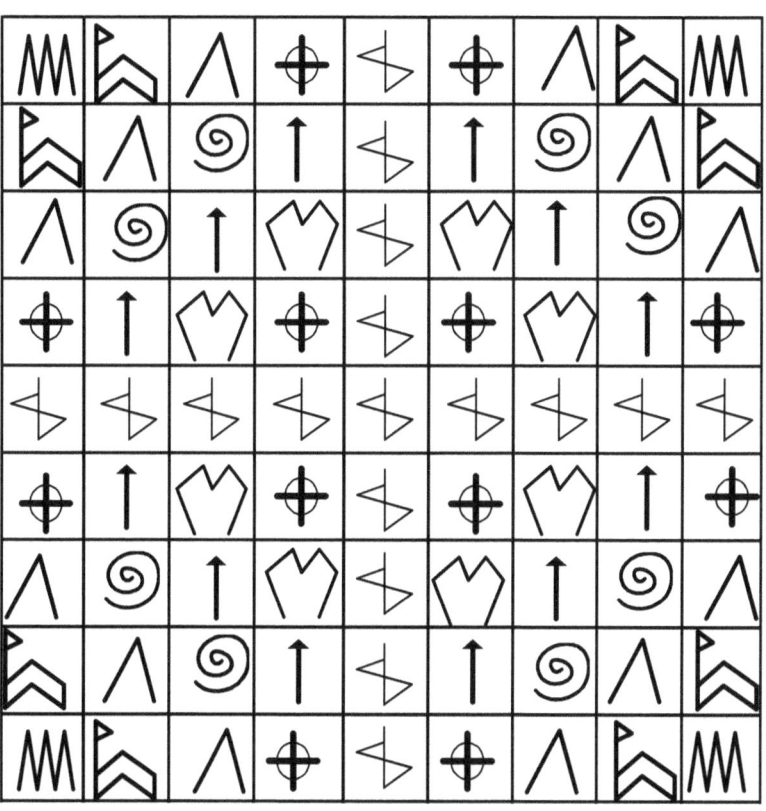

Mairt

U	R	F	U	I	U	F	R	U
R	F	C	Q	I	Q	C	F	R
F	C	Q	A	I	A	C	C	F
U	Q	A	U	I	U	A	Q	U
I	I	I	I	I	I	I	I	I
U	Q	A	U	I	U	A	Q	U
F	C	Q	A	I	A	Q	C	F
R	F	C	Q	I	Q	C	F	R
U	R	F	U	I	U	F	R	U

Baidh

The Third Grade - Druid

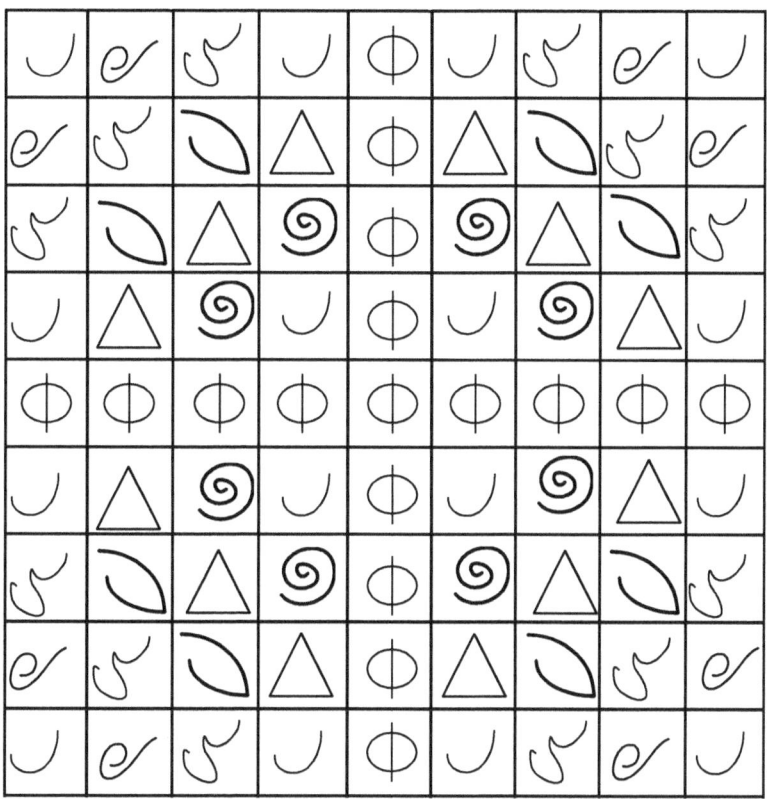

Baidh

N	B	ᴍ	B	O	B	ᴍ	B	N
B	ᴍ	ᴛ	h	O	h	ᴛ	ᴍ	B
ᴍ	ᴛ	h	ʌ	O	ʌ	h	ᴛ	ᴍ
B	h	ʌ	B	O	B	ʌ	h	B
O	O	O	O	O	O	O	O	O
B	h	ʌ	B	O	B	ʌ	h	B
ᴍ	ᴛ	h	ʌ	O	ʌ	h	ᴛ	ᴍ
B	ᴍ	ᴛ	h	O	h	ᴛ	ᴍ	B
N	B	ᴍ	B	O	B	ᴍ	B	N

Grian

The Third Grade - Druid

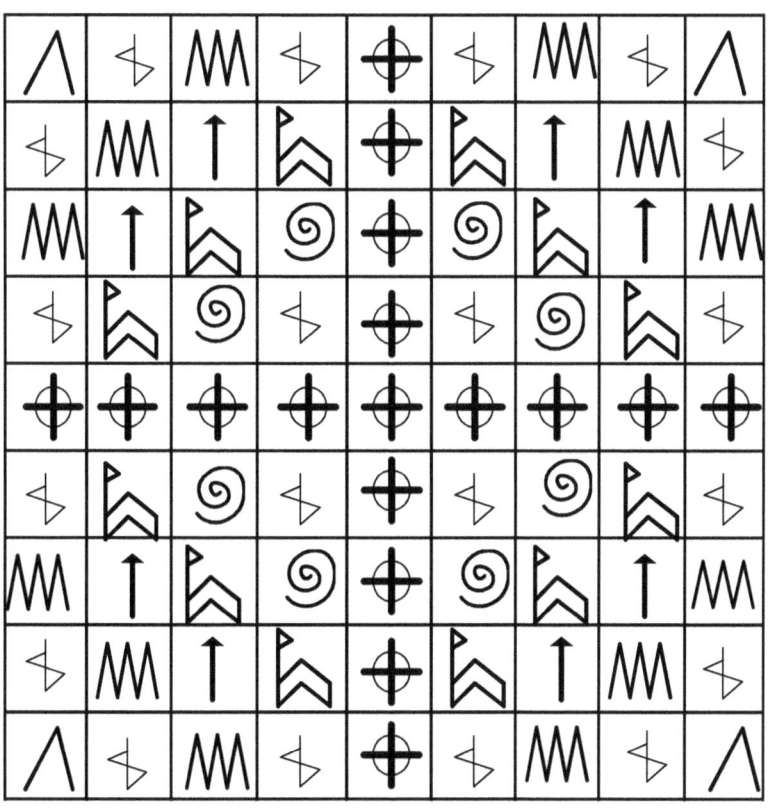

Grian

1	C	R	G	U	G	R	C	1
C	R	F	q	U	q	F	R	C
R	F	q	A	U	A	q	F	R
G	q	A	G	U	G	A	q	G
U	U	U	U	U	U	U	U	U
G	q	A	G	U	G	A	q	G
R	F	q	A	U	A	q	F	R
C	R	F	q	U	q	F	R	C
1	C	R	G	U	G	R	C	1

Luan

The Third Grade - Druid

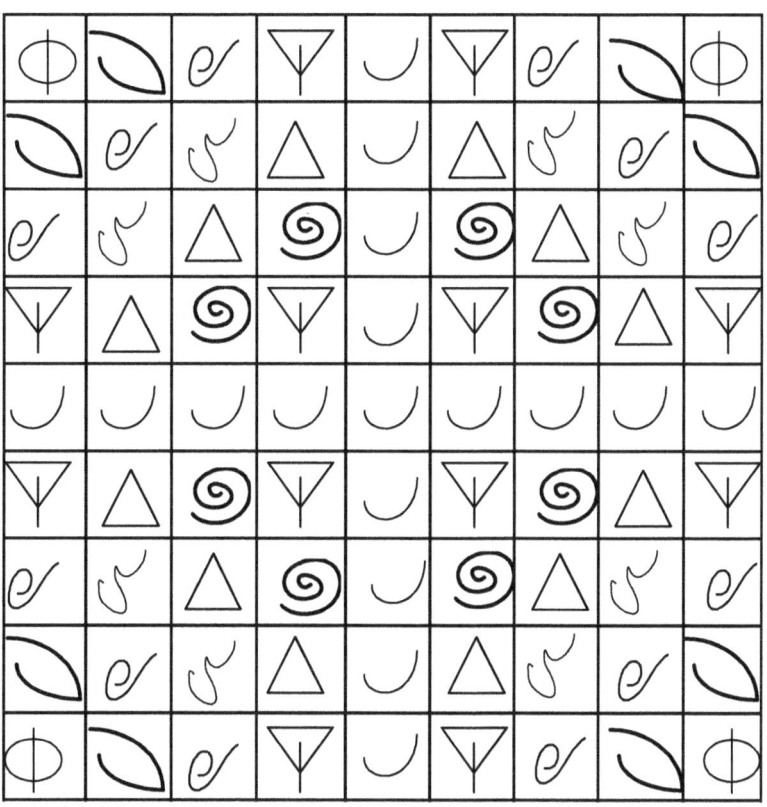

Luan

C	L	N	O	h	O	N	L	C
L	N	B	C	h	C	B	N	L
N	B	C	A	h	A	C	B	N
O	C	A	O	h	O	A	C	O
h	h	h	h	h	h	h	h	h
O	C	A	O	h	O	A	C	O
N	B	C	A	h	A	C	B	N
L	N	B	C	h	C	B	N	L
C	L	N	O	h	O	N	L	C

Domhnall

The Third Grade - Druid

Domhnall

L	B	T	O	M	O	T	B	L
B	T	H	N	M	N	H	T	B
T	H	N	A	M	A	N	H	T
O	N	A	O	M	O	A	N	O
M	M	M	M	M	M	M	M	M
O	N	A	O	M	O	A	N	O
T	H	N	A	M	A	N	H	T
B	T	H	N	M	N	H	T	B
L	B	T	O	M	O	T	B	L

Sathurn

The Third Grade - Druid

Sathurn

A	S	Z	S	E	S	Z	S	A
S	Z	S	Ng	E	Ng	S	Z	S
Z	S	Ng	N	E	F	Ng	S	Z
S	Ng	I	A	E	A	O	Ng	S
E	E	E	E	E	E	E	E	E
S	Ng	O	A	E	A	I	Ng	S
Z	S	Ng	N	E	F	Ng	S	Z
S	Z	S	Ng	E	Ng	S	Z	S
A	S	Z	S	E	S	Z	S	A

Teachdaire

Teachdaire

Of the Table of the Amhran

This table partakes of the notes of all the seven Wanderers. Care must be taken in its use as it is of tremendous power. Its main function is to bring balance unto all things and to return the three worlds to their true position in the Song.

Thus it should not be used for mundane works but rather the highest of spiritual purposes. It uniteth things that are meant to be but will stop short of creating change if none is meant to be.

Thus it would be used for resolving disputes between tribes, curing discord.

Of healing potions and herbs

A word of warning on this section. Some plants and barks are toxic even in small doses. It is worthwhile checking this before hand. The plant would tell you that such a part of it was good for healing but it often will not tell you the dose - even if you ask it. For example the juice of foxglove is good for those with weak blood pressure, however it is a poison that will stop your heart unless you take even the most minute dose. It is always worthwhile investing in a good book on botany and a herbal as a backup to your work. Remember trees do have their off days where they respond to discord and they might just lie to you.

There are two different types of healing potions the infusion by water and the infusion with wine. Infusion by water is for illnesses of the mind and infusion with wine is used for illnesses of the body.

In an infusion the appropriate plant or tree is selected by the Druid using the body of knowledge that has been developed through his own research. A person who knows the note and shape of a particular plant should also ask what its healing qualities are. Material should be collected from the tree in the usual manner. Not more than the digit of the patient's index finger should be used in the infusion.

Prepare thy space in the ancient manner.

Prepare a cauldron of water or wine on the new moon if you

are trying to draw some sort of cure towards the patient or on the full of the moon if trying to make something go away. The size of the cauldron should be big enough to fit the fist of the afflicted person comfortably.

Let the Druid gaze upon the face of the water as it heats on the fire and let him in his mind's eye see the person cured of their malady.

Then let him stand in the position of creation with the herb in his right hand.

Let him have prepared a poem of power for the herb let him recite it now.

Afterwards, let him draw the seal of plant in the air on the appropriate planetary tablet for the afflicted person and let him see it move into the water. Then gently sing the note of the plant upon the appropriate tablet for the afflicted person until the water or wine boils.

Then say:-

Creature of Bith I sacrifice thee that thy healing force shall transform this fluid into healing from the Amhran.

Place the Herb into the boiling water or wine and remove from the fire. Stir thrice and wait until cool and then place in a bottle with a stopper. The potion should be taken in a dose at the same time every day. During an hour before and unto an hour afterwards the afflicted should take only water.[1]

Of the bone and the tree

The potency of thy potions shall be increased three fold by passing them through a hollowed out bone of an animal of which thou hast been before. This bone, which should be inscribed with thy name in Ogham, should be thrust into a block of wood which is attributed to the Wanderer under which the sufferer was born. The wood which must be in depth no more than two fingers and should be inscribed with the name of the Wanderer. The bone should be

---

[1] In the case of some of the more bitter herbs or barks it was acceptable to add a spoonful of honey.

allowed to project out of it. The bone should be as broad and long as possible to facilitate the passing of the fluid.

[This is a truly phallic object which would be bound to get the Freudians excited. They would say that it was implying that you, the owner of the bone, was having sex with the patient who is the owner of the wood and passing your power in the form of semen onto them. It seems to work. C.R.]

Sacred Fire

Fire is a physical representation of the Ather and as such holds a special place among Druids. It is said that the heart of the fire moveth a man's mind unto the plane of Mag Mor itself. What we see as fire is but the liberation of that part of the Ather which layeth dormant in the material burning. After the fire has departed the corpse, or ash, of the material is a testament to how much of the Ather is within all things

Because something as holy as the Ather cannot be destroyed it transcends into another part of the Song of Creation - it endows the air and the earth around with warmth. The more of the Ather which is contained within a fire the more smoke it giveth off. This is because the radiant energy is so intense it carries more of the sooty body with it. A fire of dry wood giveth off the minimum of smoke because much of the energy hath already departed.

A bonfire or torch instantly opens a vortex to Tir Andoman, which can be used to skry. However the shape of the energy prevents creatures from entering Bith. Placing an object into a fire is akin to placing it into those parts of Tir Andoman that respond most to the Ather. This makes the art of the blacksmith a holy one for he is constantly placing the metal of Bith (which is feared by creatures in Tir Andoman) through a portal of fire into that land as part of his forging process.

Two fires placed together act like unto the staves of the Pendragons. They open up a vortex of energy which any living creature passeth between shall find their own Ubh of Fire invigorated.

Thus in some parts of Britain the Druids performed rites of passing between two fires or driving cattle between them on

Beltane. This was in past times stated as being for fertility, and indeed it can have that effect, but it is more likely to strengthen the Ubh of Fire with the virtues of the Ather.

Remember where there are two there is a third. In this case the third is the Ather and it is his energy that washes over those who walk betwixt the bonfires.

Now the Druids would especially consecrate these fires unto the note of the Ather to re-enforce this power. Sticks of hazel would be placed among the pyres. Animals and other sacrifices would be also similarly placed so that by their sacrifice the portal would open in strength.

Passing around the bonfire thrice by the priest or congregation would also place the fire deeper into Tir Andoman where it was more likely to find the presence of the Ather.

Fire is also a great purifier because before it much discord flees - particularly a holy consecrated fire. For not only is it a symbol of the Ather but also, by virtue of the sacrifice of the timber, is also a meet token of the Amhran. Discord may not thrive where such a holy fire is kindled and if such a being is touched by such a fire it would do him great harm.

The act of keeping a sacred fire burning in a temple or grove had the effect of sustaining a link unto the realm of the Ather and keeping it holy. Such fires were maintained in all the main colleges of Druidry and in most of the major temples or groves. Indeed when such had to be moved, the flame was kept in a lantern or torch and carried to the new location so that the temple's gateway to the realm of Mag Mor was not lost.

Likewise, common people would attempt to keep a fire burning in their house which was lit from the sacred flame. This was done for 'luck' but also to drive away 'evil spirits' or creatures of discord. If such a fire were to go out, then it would be renewed from the fires of the Priest who oversaw the village or relit from the bonfires of Beltane which also had the same attribution.

However once in the home of a person it represented the combined power of the family and should never be given unto another. To do this would give power over that family — thus a person asking for fire was suspected of using magic to do the family harm. They were referred to the Druid for help who in giving them fire would link them to the spirit of the tribe. However if no such fire was available they would demand that the person bring an oatcake or some sort of wheat cake which would be burnt in the fire being given and then thrown into a cauldron of water. This represented the act of going into Tir Andoman and finding their own source of fire and thus separated it from the fire in the rest of the house.

> *These days it is hard to have such a sacred fire burning, however I have a lamp that I have kept faithfully stocked with oil, which I lit from the last Beltane fire rite performed by the Order. I keep it in the room I use for my meditations and the family are under strict instructions never to let it go out. It is a devil when you move house, but its transfer has always bought a sense of history with it. My family has adopted my lamp as a tradition of its own. It is the last thing to leave the old house and the first to arrive in the new one. I have ordered that in my Will it will remain with the person who overseas the 'family house' (in this case my son) and it will probably not go out for many years after my death.* C.R.

There are two types of fire. There is the need fire and then there is the force fire.

A need fire is generally is used in a rite. It works much like the Pendragons to provide energy. The Pendragons draw energy from the Emerald Heart of the Earth while the need fire draweth it from the kingdom of the Ather.

To create a need fire thou shalt take two pieces of wood from an appropriate tree. These should be as dry as possible. One should be shaped as a pole and the other should have a hole in which the other can be inserted. The Druid shall hold the pointed stick in an upright position and twirl it rapidly unto the wood starteth to spark. As soon as it does thou should place the fungus of the Birch in flakes upon the spark until the flame rises. This is the liberation of the Ather from dead and the fire provideth the energy for the construction of thy rite.

The need fire should be built before the sun rises and lit during the first hour of the dawn.

To use a need fire and the power of the Pendragons as thou hast been taught createth much force. For that which is above is joined with that which is below.

Force fire (Tin-egin) is for more important rites that affect a nation and a community. It works on the principle that there is something wrong with the energy that a community has which is causing illness, plague or some other form. This may have degenerated until it has become a living entity or Fear (see the missive entitled 'Creatures of Discord').

Firstly all the fires in the community which suffers from discord must be put out. This removes the fuel for the Discord. A group of people must be selected to attend the rite. Each one shall representeth the distance that the rite shall include. Thus the man who liveth far unto the North shall represent the Northmost boundaries of the circle and he that liveth to the South the Southern tip. The ideal number for this rite is 27 (three to the power of three) but 9 or three is also acceptable. No man who hath committed a serious crime may take part in the rite unless his honour has been restored either by recompense or punishment.

The Force fire is lit by taking two planks of wood which are rubbed together in teams of three until the fire is produced in the manner of a need fire, the smaller the teams, the smaller the planks of wood. If only nine men are used they should be in teams of three and if three men only one. They should rub until they are exhausted and then be replaced by the other team.

Once the planks are afire they should be used to light a pyre made from nine sticks or logs of hazel. Once the fire is lit the Druid should place the shape of the fear on a stick of oak with its name in Ogham. Then chanting the name of the Amhran he should plunge it into the force fire.

The creature is drawn to the area by the fire, but finding it a holy blaze is wont to avoid it. However he is caught by his name infused on the stick of Saturn and in being cast on the fire is destroyed by the power of the Ather.

When this happens the logs are removed and plunged into nine, three or one cauldrons of water; one stick for each cauldron. The ashes of the logs are then taken unto the sea where they must be placed in a sack weighted by a stone and sunk as deep as possible.

As for the water it should be taken around to the homes of the men who took part in the rite and sprinkled around their property, this shall prevent the fear from returning for at least a year but not more than nine.

The hoop of flames

This was a rite to heal one whose Ubh of Fire had been damaged. Now you would have learnt to use the twin Pendragons to do this, but there is also another way which infuses the Ubh with the spiritual energy of the Ather rather than that of the Amhran. The reason you would use that of the Ather instead is when the person's spirit is low and requireth more to fight. The Amhran energy balanceth but addeth not to a person's stock. This rite also removeth the possibility of Faery enchantment.

Taketh thou an iron hoop of some size and wrap about it a rope of straw. Soak this with oil and set it afire. Pass the sick person through the flames or have them jump through it thrice while the Druid singeth the name of the Ather.

Then say:

> *By flame*
> *By Iron*
> *By Song*
> *By Blessing*
> *Thy Ubh is restored.*

This rite actually can be performed by the Druids for themselves if a chance encounter with the Faery or other being has left them weak. It may also be performed before significant rites to renew thy store of energy.

Fire rite of protection

This rite was used during Beltine as part of the ordinary rites, but it may be used at any time of the year, or upon moving house.

Cut thou a square of turf and set it aside leaving a square of grass free in the centre.

Make up an egg for each person whom thou wisheth to be protect painting it with the colours of their Ubh of Fire. Place these in the heart of a fire made from woods from the seven trees of creation.

Light the fire and pour much wine on the ground.

Draw before the fire a shape representing the person on all seven tablets of the book saying:

The powers of [the Wanderer] *shall protect* [name of person] *and his house*

Then when all seven words from each of the tablets are sung then say:

By the powers of the Ather let it be so.

Sing the note of the Ather.

After the fire is burnt out spread the ashes in the earth and cover the turf as the ground heals, so shall the power of protection grow.

Of the Song of the Ather

This was mostly used when the need fire was kindled. Its prime ability is to counter the evil eye or negative forces as they are now known.

The Eye of the Ather
The Eye of the Golden
The Eye of the King
Pouring upon us
At each time
At each season
Gently and Generous
Glory be to thee glorious Sun
Face of the Ather

Of the jumping through the flames

It is a long tradition amongst Celtic peoples that jumping a need or force fire will bring thee fertility or good luck. This tradition has for its roots the belief in the fires of the Druids and their ability to purify one's Ubh of Fire with the energy of the Ather.

At the top of a sacred fire there is the flames, the smoke and the heat. Together these make the element of the pure Ather energy as expressed by the fire in combination with the sacrifice of the Amhran.

Passing through this vortex of physical and spiritual energy thrice provideth a great benefit.

However, care should not be taken to disturb the need fire with thy feet for this will destroy the purposes of thy rite.

Of creatures of discord

As humankind created Gods and Goddesses so were creatures of discord born of their fears. These are beings that dwell in Tir Andoman but also in Bith because the fear and belief of them never truly departed from among men. Some are corruptions of nature spirits and others are just the raw fear from the nightmares of men. However they have a reality and their presence should not be dismissed as irrational. When such creatures appear in Bith, the work of the Druid is to remove such beings of discord and banish them to Tir Andoman where they may do no harm, save as a memory.

However they may not be destroyed as such, for nothing is ever forgotten by the Oinacos and may one day break free from Tir Andoman if the fears of humanity that bred them are not quelled by their absence from the world of men.

There are distinct breeds of these fears. The breeds of corrupted nature spirits are:

gnomes, hob-goblins, goblins, and trolls.

The breeds of fears are:

ghosts, death, plagues, unknown, storm, war, pain, poverty and famine.

Note that all of these discordant corruptions are but negative sides of positive creatures or forces which have created species that feed off humanity's fears.

Of nature spirits

Gnomes

These are corruptions of Earth elementals which are given form by personification. They are of nuisance value to a home and are rarely seen in Nature. They are usually seen as small human forms and are renowned for stealing small objects. They are created when an individual in the home refuses to accept responsibility for his own minor mistakes and blame it on a spirit. After a while the spirit removeth itself from the person's Ubh of Fire and develosp a life of his own. Since their owner believed that something was thieving from them it will inevitably start to steal such objects, generally taking such objects to Tir Andoman.

Hobgoblins

These spirits are found in nature or in the home and delight in playing mad pranks upon humans. They sometimes play musical instruments and answer those that call them with laughter. Some households are happy to become familiar with their Hobgoblin and it taketh the form of a lesser god for them. In such cases a Hobgoblin's nature can be redeemed.

But if such creatures are of malicious desire and they will often seek the destruction of the body and soul of humans. They often have the power to overtake the body or mind of a human temporarily and cause them to do violence.

They are created by intense emotion, usually of a child, who has created them to be a companion. Once created they will act independently but with the emotion of the child who created him. Like gnomes, they will often pick up or steal objects but with the sole aim of creating discord. They will throw or break objects, particularly if such breakages will cause argument. They feed off emotion either of fear or of anger.

They may also take control of a person, particularly a child and speak through them. It is also possible that they might drag a spirit from Tir Andoman who is associated with the family or region to act as a mask to create more fear. Sometimes it is hard to tell if a house is haunted by an ancestor or a hobgoblin.

In Nature, Hobgoblins thrive on places where there is fear, terror or sadness. It is because of the actions of hobgoblins that that battlefields, graveyards, prisons, gallows are such melancholy places rather than the spirits of dead ancestors. In such places there are often colonies of hobgoblins which are too weak generally to cause too much harm.

Dwarves

These live underground and rarely come to the surface. This is fortunate for they eat the flesh of men and animals and have been known to capture such for food. They are small dark men, they are tribal in nature and elect their chiefs. They are great builders and miners and were common in Scotland at one time where they lived in caves and rocks. It is said that the method of the carriage of the sacred stones of Stonehenge and Avebury was taught unto the Merlins of those days by the Dwarves.

They were not a separate race, but rather men who had decided to live underground to escape the great ices. But the time underground, without the light of the sun, gradually corrupted their souls until they were assayed by the discord. At various times they have attempted to integrate amongst normal men but despite the attempts of the Druids they were shunned.

The last recorded meeting of a Druid and a Dwarf was in the 15th century and it seems that their race had all but died of a plague contracted by eating a woman who had been afflicted and they knew the illness not.

Goblins

These are rarer and are hardly ever found near humans. These are faery who have become so corrupted by the discord that even their own kind would have them no more. Some may have been cast out for falling from grace with the King and Queen. All of them have been corrupted and twisted before they are banished from Tir Andoman. They rarely form bands and are usually solitary. As such they will rarely attack a human unless he is sick or unwell. Although one might feel some sympathy for such creatures, who are doomed to spend the song wandering the earth, they are so corrupted that it is difficult for them to ever change.

They kill animals and livestock to feed and tear them apart with their bare hands.

Trolls

Trolls are nature spirits generally associated with rocks and mountains which have been twisted by human fears and fancy. They are associated with difficult cliff faces and mountain paths and are legendary for causing rock slides. Other species are created from corrupted Water Sprites and dwell in rivers, particularly rapids. They are responsible for grabbing boats and sailors and drowning them. They only have power to do so because a person will have associated that particular place with danger and death and probably given it a name.

Of the Fears

Fears are entities that are created by humans. They can take on Godlike proportions and are extremely dangerous. Some, like ghosts, are built on genuine existing substance. But many are just built on an irrational impulse that builds a momentum until it is given life by the Amhran. Some are short lived as the fear passeth away but others last for many years.

Of ghosts the Order's teaching in the Ovate grade is already given much emphasis. However the fear of such a being gives it considerably more power. To destroy them one must find the seed of the original ancestor, its name and send it back to Tir Andoman by drawing its shape upon the tablet of the Andoman and ordering it to remain there.

If a fear possesseth but one man then find out what his fear is attributed unto. For example if it is a death fear then thou would use the Saturn page of the book of the Amhran, draw his shape upon it, sing his note and then draw it upon the square of the Andoman. This fuses the energy of the man unto the healing energy of the Amhran.

A fear will appear as a shape of dark or grey mist. It has a discordant jagged sound which respondeth to the Ubh of Fire which vibrates likewise. Thus the man who experiences the fear is soon in its possession and will act accordingly to its will.

A Fear empowered by one man will possess another and then

it will be twice as powerful. This goes on incrementally until 50 shall be possessed. Then its power is at the highest it shall attain and its power becometh spread thinner. Thus if 1,000 men are possessed each man will not be as affrightened as the original 50. However from fifty people a whole nation can be caught in the grip of the Fear.

Some fears are more powerful than others as they work with the human ability to make unto themselves unwell. The Fear of plague and pestilences feed off a tribe or village until there is not a person standing. An epidemic of even the most minor illness is spread by the fear of catching the sickness rather than any malignant humours in the air.

[In other words if you fear that you will catch someone's cold, you almost certainly will. If a larger number of people fear that a cold is in the air the Fear of the cold will gain in power and before you know it the whole country is sneezing and wheezing. In modern times we associate these illnesses with bacteria and viruses, however the two ideas are compatible. If a fear's Ubh of Fire is extensive, these bacteria and viruses are part of its physical body. We name these Fears 'strains of illness' and they have a life span as people become immune and not frightened by that strain any longer. C.R.]

A Druid should not attempt to fight a fear directly for it is too strong, being built of the Ubh of Fire of too many people. The only way to deal with a Fear is to help a tribe counter it with hope. It is for this reason that fire festivals were used to counteract pestilence and grand rites were held where the Gods were called to sooth any terrors. If enough of the Tribe believed that the rite was effective then they would unconsciously remove their link to the fear and it would die. A village need fire, by its focus on the light of the Ather, can cast out any fear.

Other fears, such as a fear of earthquakes, the sky falling or something else rare will gradually die away with the passage of time.

A Druid should be without fear so that he or she may be of service to those who are fearful. Each personal fear must be faced in its full discordant form so that when it is encountered on a grand scale its attacks fall off thy Ubh of Fire like water off a duck.

Note that a Hope, which is the converse of a Fear, may be created to forge an expectation of well being that will prevent any wide spread Fear from developing. It was for this reason that the Druids had public rites at every quarter so that people would believe the Gods and Goddesses would protect them. Any fear would have difficulty starting among those who were truly faithful. Alas no human can be truly faithful to a being that fails to encompass all his or her needs, so occasionally a fear used to spread.

Rite of the Druid

This rite has a larger cast, and required much rehearsal. Three months before a Druid's initiation he or she would be given lines to learn. I have included a copy of one of these sheets of paper so it is clear how the Druid was informed without revealing too much. They were expected to be word and action perfect, a standard which was always achieved. If the rite has to be done inside (which I do not recommend), you can replace the fires with candles. But since Fire is a crucial part of the working, you would be missing much if you do not have the fires and the torches. The purpose of the rite is to take the powers of the planets or wanderers and to integrate them into your Ubh of Fire. By taking these qualities you have power over those aspects of yourself and Nature. It builds a strong Ubhather over the Ubmather of the candidates building a being of much more power and is able to achieve so much more using the powers of the Note.

The Guardian of the Notes of the Planet would establish the notes of the candidate calculated using their Order name in relation to the page of the Book of Amhran. They would also have worked out a shape for them. This would be drawn in the Ubh of Fire of the candidate during the rite while the song of that page was sung. Thus my name in the order might be Rowan of Loxley. As I approached the Guardian of the Note of

Domhnall (Jupiter) he would sing the following note: H,N,O,H,O,N,H (with the musical notes A,C,C,A,C,C,A) and draw the following shape.

A seal performed in Jupiter.

But the Guardian of Sathurn (Saturn) would sing M,T,O,M,A,T,M (with the notes B,A,C,B,A,B) while drawing the same shape.

Rulers of the Plain of Fire.

All Druids, including Rulers of the Cave should wear Torcs, and eggs and carry their staffs.
Merlin: Pendragon bracelets, Torc, Staff of Oak, Lit torch in the ground.
White Pendragon: White Pendragon staff, a spear, Lit torch in the ground.
Red Pendragon: Red Pendragon staff, a cauldron, Lit torch in the ground.

The Third Grade - Druid

Amhran : With seven stringed harp, mirror of Bronze, hooded lamp, and cloak.
Warden of the Note of Mairt: Lit torch in the ground
Warden of the Note of Baidh: Lit torch in the ground
Warden of the Note of Teachdaire: Lit torch in the ground
Warden of the Note of Domhnall: Lit torch in the ground
Warden of the Note of Sathurn: Lit torch in the ground

The candidate should be given a bowl of milk to drink while they wait and should be placed out of earshot of the rite. They should wear their druid's egg and have their personal staff, a sword and a green lantern. The Plane of Fire should be established thus:

The Setting Aside

Amhran walks to the Merlin who hands him a dagger of Gold. Amhran then walks behind him and in a clockwise circle that encloses the whole rite (excluding the candidate) thrice. As this is done he says:-

> *I set aside this place in Bith.*
> *I set aside this place in the Tir Andoman.*
> *I set aside this place in Mag Mor.*
> *In this Kingdom Time is Not*
> *In this Kingdom Light and Darkness are Not*
> *In this Kingdom All things are Oinacos*
> *I seal this place with the Ring-Pass-Not of Gold*
> *I seal this place in the Name of the Mather*
> *I seal this place in the Name of the Ather.*
> *I seal this place in the Name of the Song which binds.*

Amhran gives the Knife of Gold to the Merlin and goes before the Altar.
> *He plays a scale on the Harp.*

Merlin: (striking staff): *The riddle is born. I am one and alone, yet I Create Three. Who am I?*

White Pendragon: *Light*

Red Pendragon: *Dark*

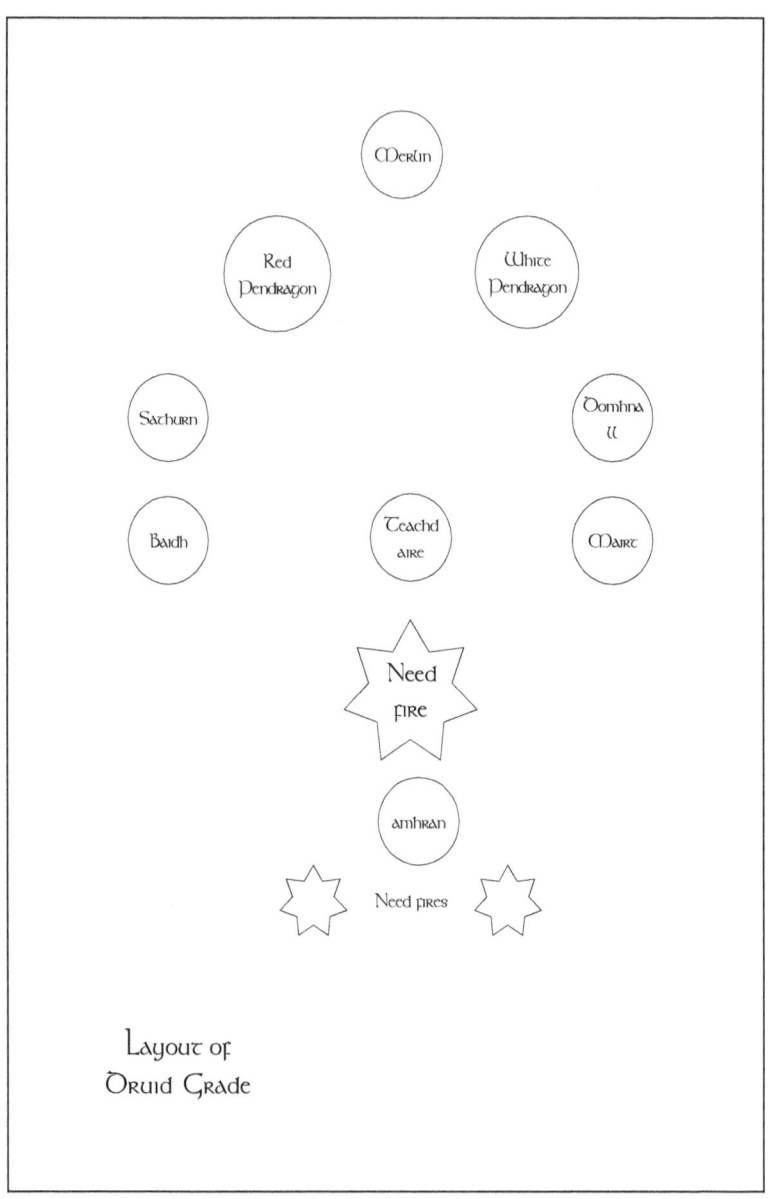

Layout of Druid Grade

Amhran: *Thou art the circle of fire. Thou art the Night's dark sky pricked with the Light of the Stars.*

Merlin: *How did I create?*

White Pendragon: *With the White Pendragon of Fire.*

Red Pendragon: *With the Red Pendragon of Water.*

Amhran: *Taking both Pendragons entwined in thy arms you created the first Breath and the first Stone.*

Merlin raises arms in the Position of Creation and then crashes bracelets together and then sings:

OOOOOOOOOOOOOOOOOOOOOOOOOOOOOOO
UUUUUUUUUUUUUUUUUUUUUUUUUUUUUUU
EEEEEEEEEEEEEEEEEEEEEEEEEEEEEEEEE

As he sings OOOOOO so does the White Pendragon sing OOOOOOOOOO. When he sings UUUUUUUU likewise does the Red Pendragon sing UUUUUUUUUUUU and when EEEEEEEEEE Amhran sings EEEEEEEEEEE.

Merlin: *Why doest I create?*

White Pendragon: *For it is thine own self*

Red Pendragon: *To Name thyself*

Amhran: *To hold a perfect image of thyself to know who thou art.*

Merlin: *Show me my image*

Amhran plays seven notes. Then when he is finished he holds up his mirror and says:-

Amhran: *Behold the Song and the Singer.*

All take their staffs and knock three times three on the ground. The Amhran plays the scale of seven notes.

The Rite

Merlin: *We are born of fire and unto the fire we shall return, carrying the light of our knowledge with us into the blackness of the Unknown.*

Amhran: *Knowledge that lights the face of the reflection of the Oinacos and reveals the purpose of my creation.*

Merlin: *What is my reflection.*

Amhran: *Humanity for all things divine are summed up in a single being.*

Merlin: *And what is a human?*

Amhran: *Seven notes and a spark.*

Merlin: *What do I see before me?*

Amhran: *The seven notes of a man who has passed many tests to come before thee; one whose destiny has taken him through the world of Bith, into the caves of Tir Andoman. One who hath found the Emerald Heart of the World and useth it as a lamp to light his way into the world of Mag Mor.*

Merlin: *Then let his adventures continue. Bring this [man/woman] into Tir Ain even unto Mag Mor. Let [him/her] meet and merge with the notes of his being.*

The Amhran goes forth to the candidate while the need fires are lit in the ancient manner. The candidate must approach with this green lamp lit and held upright with his right hand and his staff in his left. He is led to stand between the need fires.

Merlin: *Who is it that stands between the purifying fires of the Ather?*

Ovate: *I do.*

Merlin: *Who art thou?*

Ovate: *I was a rock*
   I was a tree
   I was a fox
   I was a man
   I was a woman
   I was a farmer
   I was warrior
   I endured the three-fold death

The Third Grade - Druid

*I spoke unto the Gods and Goddesses
I wrested the Emerald Heart of the World from the Crown of the Mather.*

Merlin: *Why didest thou do these things?*

Ovate: *To fulfil the Song of the Amhran.*

Merlin: *Doest thou know where thou art?*

Ovate: *The Emerald Heart of the World hath brought me unto this plane of Fire, the domain of the Ather.*

Merlin: *What seeketh thou here?*

Ovate: *I seeketh the balance to the Mather so that the Song may spring forth from my breast and I might be a true reflection of the One Thing.*

Merlin: *Then let thou faceth the notes of creation and merge these into thy being.*

Amhran leads Ovate to the Note of Sathurn

Sathurn: *Submit to my power which is death.*

Ovate (prompted): *I have died many times and each time been reborn. Therefore thou has no power unless I give it to thee. Therefore I take thy power unto my own.*

Instructed by the Amhran he takes the sword and holds it to the throat of Sathurn.

Sathurn: *My head is thine. I give thee my power and Note.*

Sings his note of Ovate and draws sign into his or her Ubh of Fire.

Ovate: (prompted): *I have died many times and each time been reborn. Therefore thou hath no power unless I give it thee. Therefore I take thy power unto my own.*

Instructed by the Amhran he takes the sword and holds it to the throat of Sathurn.

Sathurn: *My head is thine. I give thee my power and Note.*

Sings his note of Ovate and draws sign into his or her Ubh of Fire.

Amhran leads the candidate to the Note of Baidh

Baidh: *Submit to my power, which is Lust.*

Ovate: (prompted): *I have lusted and loved. Therefore thou hath no power unless I give it thee. Therefore I take thy power unto my own.*

Instructed by the Amhran he takes the sword and holds it to the throat of Baidh.

Baidh: *My head is thine. I give thee my power and Note.*

Sings his note of Ovate and draws sign into his or her Ubh of Fire.

Amhran leads the candidate to the Note of Mairt

Mairt: *Submit to my power, which is Violence.*

Ovate: (prompted): *I have killed and I have created. Therefore thou hath no power unless I give it thee. Therefore I take thy power unto my own.*

(Instructed by the Amhran he takes the sword and holds it to the throat of Mairt.)

Mairt: *My head is thine. I give thee my power and Note.*

Sings his note of the Ovate and draws sign into his or her Ubh of Fire.

Amhran leads the candidate to the Note of Teachdaire

Teachdaire: *Submit to my power, which is lies.*

Ovate: (prompted): *I have lied and I have spoken the Song. Therefore thou hath no power unless I give it thee. Therefore I take thy power unto my own.*

Instructed by the Amhran he takes the sword and holds it to the throat of Teachdaire.

Teachdaire: *My head is thine. I give thee my power and Note.*

Sings his note of the Ovate and draws sign into his or her Ubh of Fire.

Amhran leads Ovate to the White Pendragon

White Pendragon: *Submit to my power, which is Despotism.*

Ovate (prompted): *I have been a despot and a wise ruler. Therefore thou hath no power unless I give it thee. Therefore I take thy power unto my own.*

Instructed by the Amhran he takes the sword and holds it to the throat of White Pendragon.

White Pendragon: *My head is thine. I give thee my power and Note.*

Sings his note of Ovate and draws sign of Domhnall into his or her Ubh of Fire.

Amhran leads the candidate to the Red Pendragon

Red Pendragon: *Submit to my power, which is delusion and illusion.*

Ovate (prompted): *I have been deluded and I have dreamed the truth. Therefore thou hath no power unless I give it thee. Therefore I take thy power unto my own.*

Instructed by the Amhran he takes the sword and holds it to the throat of Red Pendragon.

Red Pendragon: *My head is thine. I give thee my power and Note.*

Sings his note of the Ovate and draws sign of Luan into his or her Ubh of Fire.

Amhran leads the Ovate to before the central needfire.

Amhran: *Submit to my power, which is arrogance.*

Candidate (prompted): *I have been arrogant and I have seen the spirit of nature. Therefore thou has no power* unless I give it thee. Therefore I take thy power unto my own.

He takes the sword and holds it to the throat of Amhran.

Amhran: *My head is thine. I give thee my power and Note.*

(Sings his note of the Ovate and draws sign of Grian into his or her Ubh of Fire.)

The Notes form a circle about the candidate with their torches and sing their notes facing him or her. Then they turn outwards and sing their notes.

Notes: *We serve* [Ovate's Order name] *our virtues and vices are his (hers).*

Amhran: *Notes of* [Ovate's Order name] *form thy position in the Song.*

The Notes form an astrological chart of the candidate with the first house facing the Merlin.

Amhran: *Mighty Merlin I present unto you the Song of* [Ovate's Order name].

Merlin: (Enters the state of Oneness of the One Thing). *Bring it forth that I may know.*

Amhran: (To Ovate). *Thy journey is over. I am thee and thou art me. It is now thy time to reflect the One Thing.*

Amhran hands Ovate his double-sided mirror and then from behind him leads him to face the Merlin who has stood behind the candidate. The Amhran helps him to hold the Mirror to the face of the Merlin (and thus his or her own face).

Merlin:
I was a rock
I was a tree
I was a fox
I was a man
I was a woman

I was a farmer
I was a warrior
I endured the three-fold death
I spoke unto the Gods and Goddesses
I wrested the Emerald Heart of the World from the Crown of the Mather.
I fought the Notes of the Amhran and liberated the Good from the Discord.
I am [Ovate's Order name]
I am the Ather
I am the Mather
I am the Amhran.
I am the One Thing.
In the whole of Creation
I have beheld my own face.
I am one and many.
I know.

With a slow turning the Merlin sits the candidate on his throne and leaving him gazing at his reflection stands behind him.

All fires and torches are extinguished[2] other than the fires of the Merlin/Candidate. There is a long pause.

Amhran: *Thou who art the embodiment of the Song, thou art the reflection of the Oinacos and thus the powers of the Universe are thine to understand. Now the Druidic Order of Pendragon names thee Druid.*

Merlin gives the candidate his Bracelets. Then in the following order the torches (not the fires) are relit. Ather, Mather, Amhran, Grian, Luan, Teachdaire, Mairt, Baidh, Domhnall and Sathurn.

Merlin (prompts the Druid): *The riddle is born. I am one and alone, yet I Create Three. Who am I?*

White Pendragon: *Light*

---

[2] Although the fires were put out and stayed out, we used hooded lanterns instead of torches and shielded them during this part of the rite. It made it easier for them to be relit.

Red Pendragon: *Dark*

Amhran : *Thou art the circle of fire. Thou art the Night's dark sky pricked with the Light of the Stars.*

Merlin (prompting Druid): *How did I create?*

White Pendragon: *With the White Pendragon of Fire.*

Red Pendragon: *With the Red Pendragon of Water.*

Amhran: *Taking both Pendragons entwined in thy arms you created the first Breath and the first Stone.*

Merlin raises the Druid's arms in the Position of Creation and then crashes bracelets together and then together they sing:

OOOOOOOOOOOOOOOOOOOOOOOOOOOOOO
UUUUUUUUUUUUUUUUUUUUUUUUUUUUUU
EEEEEEEEEEEEEEEEEEEEEEEEEEEEEEEE

As he sings OOOOOOOOOO so does the White Pendragon sing OOOOOOOOOO. When he sings UUUUUUUUUU likewise does the Red Pendragon sing UUUUUUUUUUUUUUU and when EEEEEEEEEEEEE Amhran sings EEEEEEEEEEEEE.

Merlin (prompts Druid): *Why doest I create?*

White Pendragon: *For it is thine own self*

Red Pendragon: *To Name thyself*

Amhran: *To hold a perfect image of thyself to know who thou art.*

Merlin (prompts Druid): *Show me my image*

Amhran plays seven notes and the seven notes sing their note as he or she plays them.

Merlin: *The rite is completed, the song is done and another has begun. Let the mysteries shown here be embodied in this Druid from now until the Oinacos beholds the whole of creation and the singer finishes the Song.*

The Druid is lead between the fires and departs alone into the world in silence.

The Closure

Merlin (striking staff and stands in the position of Power):
I am half man and half tree, who walks betwixt worlds whose feet touch the earth and whose hands reach heaven. Within my breast is the seed of the Oinacos. In its name I make the three Worlds one again.

[White Pendragon sings the AAAAAAAAAAAAAAAAA. Red Pendragon sings the OOOOOOOOOOOOOOOOOO. Amhran sings the UUUUUUUUUUUUUUUUUUU. This is done simultaneously].

Merlin *The riddle is answered, the rite is done the worlds are aligned. Let us depart unto our groves in peace.*

Address to the Druid on the performance of the last rite of Initiation

In the rite of initiation you have performed you have taken the last step in the Order and your first in life as a Druid. There are positions of service in the Order of Pendragon, but they add not to your personal development.

Many who have gone through the ordeals that their training within this Order has placed upon them are left with a feeling of emptiness at this point. It is as if the trellis that supported their growth as a sapling has been removed and they are feeling alone, almost cast out from the Order that has trained them.

Nothing could be further from the case as this rite and the subsequent teaching comprises the work of many lifetimes. Already you have discovered the unlimited riches of Tir Andoman, which will be the source of much wisdom and adventures for the rest of your life. Now in the realm of Mag Mor the rest of your work is symbolically shown to you and that will never stop even if you have departed Bith never to return again.

This rite differed from the others because you were required to memorise part of the rite beforehand. This is an indication of your own increasing independence from the forces that have been your guides in the previous grades.

You notice that as you entered the rite you were holding the green lantern, which indicates your spiritual attainment in attaining the Emerald Heart at the centre of the World. It might be that you only saw this in a brief vision, but it is enough to change your life to take you into the higher spiritual realms of Mag Mor.

The gates of Mag Mor are of fire and you stood between these sacred fires upon your entry into the ritual. These acted to strengthen your Ubh of Fire with the fires of the Ather that enable you to see into Mag Mor. In other words a vision of Mag Mor is only possible once you hold the Emerald Heart of the World and have raised your consciousness beyond the personality and into the cosmic levels.

When this is attained, then you have taken the energy of the Amhran, which dwells in the heart of nature and carried it to the highest aspect of creation. The pure spirit of the Ather transmutes the serpents of the Pendragon, which are united in the Emerald Light. Your body becomes transformed and every cell is over flowing with the power of the Song.

You are then ready for the next stage of the adventure, which is the challenging of the Planetary Notes. All of creation is created by the operation of these beings and yet all are affected by discord. In this level you task is to realise the importance of discord and be aware of your own resonance within it. Discord is important for it was created by the Oinacos from elements in its own self that it did not understand. The function of the Druid at this level is to realise those discordant aspects of his own self and bring them into balance.

When this work is completed the Druid realises that the discordant aspects are like the sand that creates the pearl in the oyster. When the aspects that resonate to the Oinacos realise its discordant aspects they are transformed into something glorious. Each planet creates a challenge and over coming it grants a power. You should not oppose discord, but transform it. To transform it you have to honour it, blend with it and in doing so you will see it on a higher level. From this higher level it can be redeemed.

In the rite, you will have noticed that each planet would have drawn the seal of your name as copied from the Book of Amhran. Each person's symbol will be different so this means that each Wanderer's power will be tailored for the individual.

This part of the initiation actually opened your Ubh of Fire to the influence of the planetary powers, which will make them more accessible to you. To ensure that you do not suffer too much of an imbalance towards discord, you will note that the Planetary notes stand within your Ubh of Fire with their torches facing you. These torches, as with the need fires, directly link your Ubh of Fire with the energies of the Ather and thus give you the purest most positive expression of the Planetary Note.

They then face outward to indicate that the powers of the Note are able to manifest through thy Ubh of Fire and are willing servants to your will.

Next the Notes are instructed to take their positions as they stand in your Natal chart. Your natal chart is your score in the Song, you are not required in this life time to be anything more than what your chart shows at the time you were born. The Amhran does not judge those who were unable to match the standards and skills of other men, but rather how well you matched the skills as depicted in thy chart. It would matter not if you absorbed the powers of the Wanderers and merged with the Oinacos itself in this lifetime, if you had not fulfilled who you are in accordance to your chart you would have to repeat this incarnation.

You will notice that although we make much in this grade of Astrology, we do not teach this science within the walls of this Order. There once was a time where this was so, but in these times there are many books which are more than capable and our students can find their instruction elsewhere. However we do not use the so-called 'modern astrology' that features planets beyond the limits of Saturn. We hold that as they are unable to be seen by all but the most powerful telescopes they cannot have an influence in the creation of the World, as the vibration of their notes cannot be heard on this planet. Our ancient brethren had no information about these planets and more research is needed to find how these planets fit into the Great Song of Creation[3] Let it be known that no human has ever had to integrate the powers of Hershel or

Neptune as part of their path towards the One Thing, and their discovery by 'rational astronomers' has not changed this.

We recommend the book *Christian Astrology*, by W. Lilly as an excellent introduction to the topic and the key to unlocking the astrological information in your chart.

This rite, unlike the others seems to lack the sacrifices of the other initiations. Our students often wonder about this as one of the Order's most important mottos is that nothing is ever achieved without sacrifice. In fact in this rite sacrifice is overtly present throughout the rite in the presence of the need fires and torches that burn throughout. These need fires are of woods that reflect the seven notes that built you and your creation and are thus dying to the flame throughout the rite. But more profoundly is the sacrifice that happens when face beholds face in the next part of the rite. Indeed the next part of your initiation is the one which is the most profound and from the point of view of most religions the most heretical. It effectively shows you that after you have integrated the Mather and the Ather energies and merged with the planetary notes you are the Amhran. It says that the Amhran is a direct reflection of the One Thing.

Now, while some religions speak of man or nature being made in God's image they stop short of saying that Man or Nature is the image of God. The central mystery of the Druids was this truth — when you look upon Nature you are seeing God; when you approach your fellow man you are dealing with God. And likewise because you are the reflection of God, you are in Truth God itself as is all of Nature about thee.

There is no separation between the One Thing, the Song, or the Mather and the Ather; they are all reflections of the One Thing. Likewise there is no division between thee and the rest of nature. A tree is simply you occupying another space; a beggar is simply you playing out the role of poverty, a rich man is simply you experiencing the challenges of material wealth. Thus one should not look upon another with envy or superiority because you are he too and there is no difference between you.

---

[3] This was never done and the Druids in the Order universally stuck to 'traditional astrology' of W. Lilly ignoring all modern developments including asteroids, planetary moons, Neptune, Uranus, and Pluto.

You might ask how is this realisation a sacrifice as nothing seems to be lost and yet divinity is gained. All things are sacrificed at this point of transition. You sacrifice your life in Creation to sit upon the Throne of the One Thing. The Oinacos changes in the light of your experiences and thus something old passes away. The constructs of the Ather, Mather and Amhran having achieved their purpose to answer the questions of the Oinacos also pass away. All that is left is you, the One Thing, alone in the dark on the Throne of the Oinacos and given the powers of creation. You partake in the nature and mechanics of the Creation and the knowledge and understanding that brings.

Then you departed the rite as you would depart from creation after your identification with the One Thing. There is nothing that Creation can teach you and there is no expression for the mysteries you will discover.

This departure also represents your final independence from the Order. In ancient times you would remain within the caste of Pendragon but would be sent to a village or township to practice your skills among men. You would also retire to your groves to work your magic and to realise your deep connection with the Oinacos in reality rather than in the symbolism of the Rite.

Occasionally, at times of crisis, or for the seasonal rites, you would join your fellow Pendragons to share your experiences in song, poem or in magic. However most of the path of the Druid is a lonely one in human terms. Their companionship is found among the trees, rocks, stones and animals and the ever-resounding notes of the Song.

Letter from the Merlin

Congratuations upon being selected for advancement to the Grade of Druid, which is the completion of your ritual initiation work in this Order. This rite is considerably important and requires much work from you both in terms of preparation and memorisation.

During the next three months you will be required to continue you work with the Emerald Heart of the World, which your mentor has indicated that you have glimpsed in your regular meditation work. You must achieve a considerable raport with this energy and integrate it within your Ubh of Fire. This can be done using the Raising of the Pendragons exercise immediately after your journeys to Tir Andoman for the vision of the Emerald.

You will be required at various points in the rite to speak the following phrases unprompted. These are answers to questions that need to be memorised along with the 'cue lines' to make sure that you say the right phrase and the correct time. The Phrases are:

Question: *Who is it that stands between the purifying fires of the Ather?*

Answer: *I do.*

Question: *Who art thou?*

Answer:
I was a rock
I was a tree
I was a fox
I was a man
I was a woman
I was a farmer
I was a warrior
I endured the three-fold death
I spoke unto the Gods and Goddesses
I wrested the Emerald Heart of the World from the Crown of the Mather.

Question: *Why didst thou do these things?*

Answer: *To fulfil the Song of the Amhran.*

Question: *Doest thou know where thou art?*

Answer: *The Emerald Heart of the World hath brought me unto this Plane of Fire, the domain of the Ather.*

Question: *What seeketh thou here?*

Answer: *I seeketh the balance to the Mather so that the Song may spring forth from my breast and I might be a* *true reflection of the One Thing.*

During the next few months you will notice that you will face many challenges to your discipline and some of the hardest tests during your journeys in Tir Andoman. This is part of the process of becoming a Druid, for before you are ready for the additional responsibility that is conferred upon you it is important that the Amhran test you to see that you are worthy.

This is not the act of an evil god punishing you for your sins. This 'testing' is a process where the Amhran is opening your Ubh of Fire to more powers and in the process it empowers your own tendency towards discord. It is a mercy that the Amhran does this slowly and shuts it down if the discord is too great.

No doubt you have already experienced some of this at various parts of your quest, and are already aware of what I am trying to tell you. There is no certain way of telling how you will be tested, other than the fact it is a measure of your own personal weakness and tendency towards discord, which will become the most obvious to you.

Be aware that you are being tested and that it is not one that you cannot over come. Watch the discord hatch out and realise that is part of the process. Embrace it as an aspect of yourself and accept that it comes from the Amhran. Don't fight, blame someone else, or bad fortune, what you experience is your own ability to create discord and none else. When you have dealt with it (and this may happen long after your initiation ceremony) you will receive much more power and happiness.

I wish you well for the coming months.

Chapter Five

The Rites

This first rite is for those who wish to work with the Order of the Pendragon and perhaps re-activate it. It is based on a rite called the Installation of the Merlin that was an interesting working that was carried out by the Retiring Merlin and the one who would take his place. It is not the time and place for this rite to be published, I will leave that decision in the hands of others. I saw it performed once, when my first initiator handed over the reins of power to he who would become the last Merlin. Its aim was to link the person to the powers that created the Order on the other levels of existence, for it has a presence both in Tir Andoman and Mag Mor. In Mag Mor it is said that a group of Druids and Merlin dwell to help others reach their exalted state. Rather than merging completely with the Oinacos, they step in and out of the Light where they act as beacons to those searching for the Truth. When upon Mag Mor such beings open gateways between the Plane of Fire and Tir Andoman. Their spirits appear to hold forth teaching schools in the Underworld where the souls of those who are ready join them either in meditation or in Sleep. It was to link the Order to these beings that this rite was constructed. It aims to link the group to the soul of the Druid caste of Pendragon, which has been active since time immemorial. The rite requires the four main Rulers of the Grove and ideally it should be performed as the sun rises on the Spring Equinox. This will give the newly formed order an impetus that derives from Nature. If this is not possible it can be performed any time between Spring and the Summer Solstice, it should NOT be worked afterwards as the forces of Nature will work against you.

The Rite of Contact.

Lay out the temple as the third degree diagram only without the planetary officers. The Merlin should wear the bracelets, the Red and White Pendragons should carry their staffs and the Amhran should have his harp. There should be a bonfire in the centre of the sacred space made from the seven sacred woods. Each Ruler of the Grove should carry a bottle of Wine. Light the bonfire.

The Setting Aside

Amhran walks to the Merlin who hands him a dagger of Iron. Amhran then walks behind him and in a clockwise circle that encloses the whole rite thrice. As this is done he says:-

I set aside this place in Bith.
I set aside this place in the Tir Andoman.
I set aside this place in the Mag Mor.
In this Kingdom Time is Not
In this Kingdom Light and Darkness are Not
In this Kingdom All things are Oinacos
I seal this place with the Ring-Pass-Not of Iron
I seal this place in the Name of the Mather
I seal this place in the Name of the Ather.
I seal this place in the Name of the Song which binds.

Amhran gives the Knife of Iron to the Merlin and goes before the Altar.

He plays a scale on the Harp.

Merlin:

In the name of the Oinacos
In the name of the Mather
In the name of the Ather
In the name of the Amhran
I call the creatures of Tir Andoman

> *I call the creatures of Mag Mor*
> *To witness my pledge*
> *To seal my bond*
> *To the Order of Pendragon.*

He pours wine on the ground before the bonfire. This oath is then repeated by the other Rulers of the Grove.

Merlin: *Out of our sacrifice we call the Ubhs of the Ancestors of this Order*
Be present from thy home in Tir Andoman. Pledge thy power to our Order.

Soon the area will start to be filled with the shades of the former Druids of Old. They will appear to stand in the position of power and funnel energy into the fire.

Merlin: *Out of our sacrifice we call the spiritual beings that animated our Ancestors of this Order. Be present from thy home in Mag Mor. Pledge thy power to our Order.*

Above the shades will appear beings of light and they shall network and form a wheel with spokes which meet above the fire.

Merlin: *Out of our sacrifice we call the Gods and Goddesses, whose names we remember and those whose names we have forgotten. Pledge thy power to our Order. Behind the shades will appear beings of light.*

Merlin: *Out of our sacrifice we call the Animal Kingdom. Pledge thy power to our Order.*

Behind the Gods and Goddesses the images of many animals will appear.

Merlin: *Out of our sacrifice we call the Plant Kingdom. Pledge thy power to our Order.*

Behind the Animals the images of many Trees will appear.

Merlin: *Out of our sacrifice we call the Stone Kingdom. Pledge thy power to our Order.*

Behind the trees you shall see the outline of mountains.

Merlin:
The Three Worlds are in agreement.
The Three Worlds have empowered.
The Order of Pendragon opens its doors in Mag Mor
The Order of Pendragon opens its doors in Tir Andoman
The Order of Pendragon opens its doors in Bith.

Pause

Merlin: *Oh ye spirits of Ancient Merlins form a link with me that I may hold this office in wisdom, reverence and power.*

Amhran: *Oh ye spirits of Ancient Amhran form a link with me that I may hold this office in wisdom, reverence and power.*

Red Pendragon: *Oh ye spirits of Ancient Red Pendragons form a link with me that I may hold this office in wisdom, reverence and power.*

White Pendragon: *Oh ye spirits of Ancient White Pendragon form a link with me that I may hold this office in wisdom, reverence and power.*

Allow this to happen.

Merlin (striking staff): *The riddle is born. I am one and alone, yet I Create Three. Who am I?*

White Pendragon: *Light*

Red Pendragon: *Dark.*

Amhran: *Thou art the circle of fire. Thou art the Night's dark sky pricked with the Light of the Stars.*

Merlin: *How did I create?*

White Pendragon: *With the White Pendragon of Fire.*

Red Pendragon: *With the Red Pendragon of Water.*

Amhran: *Taking both Pendragons entwined in thy arms you created the first Breath and the first Stone.*

Merlin raises arms in the Position of Creation and then crashes bracelets together and then sings:

*OOOOOOOOOOOOOOOOOOOOOOOOOOOOOO
UUUUUUUUUUUUUUUUUUUUUUUUUUUUUU
EEEEEEEEEEEEEEEEEEEEEEEEEEEEEEEE*

As he sings OOOOOOOO so does the White Pendragon sing OOOOOOOO. When He sings UUUUUUUUUU likewise does the Red Pendragon sings UUUUUUUUUUUUUUUUUU and when EEEEEEEEEEEEE Amhran sings EEEEEEEEEEEEEE.

Merlin: *Why doest I create?*

White Pendragon: *For it is thine own self*

Red Pendragon: *To Name thyself*

Amhran: *To hold a perfect image of thyself to know who thou art.*

Merlin: *Show me My image*

Amhran plays seven notes and then light the torches or lanterns on each of the stones. Then when he is finished the holds up his mirror and says:-

Amhran: *Behold the Song and the Singer.*

All take their staffs and knock three times three on the ground. The Amhran places the scale of seven notes.

Merlin: *The rite is done, the message hath passed to a new runner, the Order of Pendragon is reborn.*

The official rites

The opening and closing was the same what ever non-initiatory rite we performed. For the sake of space I have separated these so that the opening and closing are placed together. There then follows the ordinary monthly meeting rite and then those for the Equinoxes and Solstices. These would of course be placed between the opening and closing. I should point out that there were also rites for the four quarter festivals and many for special purposes. Although the ordinary monthly meeting rite was considered very important (it had to be performed at least six times a year) there were other rites that were also performed as a middle part of the ritual. One I remember particularly was the defence of the land rite that must have been one of final workings that the last Merlin performed before he was killed. This was during a time in the war when the Germans were very successfully destroying our airfields as a prelude to invasion. If it had continued there was no doubt that an invasion would have been successful. But soon after its performance the Germans switched their attacks from airfields to bombing London itself and were defeated by the aircraft they should have destroyed on the ground.

The Merlin felt the rite had gone well but said afterwards that he felt that further sacrifices were needed before the Song of Destruction ended. It would appear that the sacrifice of countless London people, including the Merlin himself might have been that price.

For the sake of space, I have not included the seasonal or special rites and will leave these to be published at a future date. They were not considered as important as the initiations or the Equinox and Solstice rites.

The grove should be set up as the first degree diagram.

Rulers of the Grove

All Druids, including Rulers of the Grove should wear normal clothes, and eggs and carry their staffs. Torches (or candles and lanterns).
Merlin: Pendragon bracelets, Torc, Staff of Oak
White Pendragon: White Pendragon staff, a spear, Hammer in belt, wine in bottle.
Red Pendragon: Red Pendragon staff. Garrotte about neck, small cauldron.

Amhran: With seven stringed harp, mirror of Bronze. Before it should be placed a bonfire made of the seven woods of creation.

The Setting Aside

Amhran walks to the Merlin who hands him a dagger of Iron. Amhran then walks behind him and in a clockwise circle that encloses the whole rite (excluding the candidate) thrice. As this is done he says:-

> *I set aside this place in Bith.*
> *I set aside this place in the Tir Andoman.*
> *I set aside this place in the Mag Mor.*
> *In this Kingdom Time is Not*
> *In this Kingdom Light and Darkness are Not*
> *In this Kingdom All things are Oinacos*
> *I seal this place with the Ring-Pass-Not of Iron*
> *I seal this place in the Name of the Mather*
> *I seal this place in the Name of the Ather.*
> *I seal this place in the Name of the Song which binds.*

Amhran gives the Knife of Iron to the Merlin and goes before the Altar.

He plays a scale on the Harp.

Merlin (striking staff): *The riddle is born. I am one and alone, yet I Create Three. Who am I?*

White Pendragon: *Light*

Red Pendragon: *Dark*

Amhran: *Thou art the circle of fire. Thou art the Night's dark sky pricked with the Light of the Stars.*

Merlin: *How did I create?*

White Pendragon: *With the White Pendragon of Fire.*

Red Pendragon: *With the Red Pendragon of Water.*

Amhran: *Taking both Pendragons entwined in thy arms you created the first Breath and the first Stone.*

Merlin raises arms in the Position of Creation and then crashes bracelets together and then sings:

*OOOOOOOOOOOOOOOOOOOOOOOOOOOOO
UUUUUUUUUUUUUUUUUUUUUUUUUUUUUU
EEEEEEEEEEEEEEEEEEEEEEEEEEEEEEEEE*

As he sings OOOOOOOO so does the White Pendragon sing OOOOOOOO. When he sings UUUUUUUUUU likewise does the Red Pendragon sings UUUUUUUUUUUUUUUUUU and when EEEEEEEEEEEEE Amhran sings EEEEEEEEEEEEEE.

Merlin: *Why doest I create?*

White Pendragon: *For it is thine own self*

Red Pendragon: *To Name thyself*

Amhran: *To hold a perfect image of thyself to know who thou art.*

Merlin: *Show me my image*

Amhran plays seven notes and then light the torches or lanterns on each of the stones. Then when he is finished the holds up his mirror and says:-

Amhran: *Behold the Song and the Singer.*

All take their staffs and knock three times three on the ground. The Amhran plays the scale of seven notes.

The closing

The Rite of Union

Merlin: *The Land is sustained. Let us now seek union with the Amhran.*

White Pendragon: *The Power of the Ather is in this place.*

Red Pendragon: *The Cauldron of the Mather encompasses us.*

White Pendragon places his wine into the Cauldron of the Mather. The Amhran walks around the bonfire clockwise and stands between the Red and White Pendragons. The Red Pendragon presents him with the Cauldron. The Merlin stands opposite him.

Merlin: *Who am I?*

Amhran: *You are the Oinacos, you are the Mather, the Ather and the Amhran.*

Merlin: *Then I am thee and thou art me*

Amhran: *I am thy heartbeat when thou shines through the depths of Nature.*
I am thy song that echoes through thine own creation.
I am thy breath in the wind
I am thy tears in the rain
I am thy warmth in a summer's day
I am thy stability in rock
I am thy growth in the tree.
I am thy power in the horse
I am thy mirror in the human

Merlin: *Then thou art my sacrifice in creation.*

Amhran: *Nothing is achieved without sacrifice.*

Merlin: *Then I shall drink of thy sacrifice Amhran so that I shall know.*

Merlin drinks from the Cauldron.

Amhran: *Let all in this Order drink of the blood of the Amhran.*
That in drinking thou shalt be bound to the Song of Creation.

Starting with the White Pendragon, then the White Pendragon, and finally the Druids in seniority all drink from the Cauldron. Then when the last has drunk the Amhran drinks from the Cauldron and says:

> *Light's sacrifice to the Dark is done*
> *The Calf quickens and grows into a bull.*
> *The cauldron fills with Song.*
> *I have died*
> *I have been reborn.*
> *In the blood of the Order*

All return to their places as in the start of the rite.

The closing of the circle.

Amhran: *The rite is done.*

Merlin (striking staff and stands in the position of Power): *I am half man and half tree, who walks betwixt worlds whose feet touch the earth and whose hands reach heaven. Within my breast is the seed of the Oinacos. In its name I make the three worlds one again.*

[White Pendragon sings the AAAAAAAAAAAAAAAA. Red Pendragon sings the OOOOOOOOOOOOOOOOOO. Amhran Sings the UUUUUUUUUUUUUUUUUU. This is done simultaneously].

> *The riddle is answered, the rite is done the worlds are aligned. Let us depart unto our groves in peace.*

The ordinary rite

Merlin stands in the position of power.

Merlin: *I call upon the ancient powers of the land to be present in this sacred Grove. Untwine thee red and white serpents from the Emerald Heart of the World. Burrow through the worlds so that through my walk along the paths and boundaries of this land, leads to the accomplishment of the song.*

The Red and the White Pendragons, along with the rest of the Order rhythmically beat their staves on the ground. After time, the Pendragons shall arise from the Emerald Heart of the Earth and rise up the wands of the Red and White Pendragons. When the Merlin senses that this has been achieved he stands in the position of creation between the Red and the White Pendragons.

Merlin:
From the Heart of the World,
I take Light and Darkness
Red and White
In perfect balance
In perfect harmony
Free from Discord
Let the paths linking this Land be united in Light

Facing East.
Let the Light of the Amhran flow to the East

Facing the South
Let the Light of the Amhran flow to the South

Facing the West
Let the Light of the Amhran flow to the West

Facing the North
Let the Light of the Amhran flow to the North

Facing the West again

Amhran: *From this place, each road becomes a linking to the Song*
This place is its heartbeat.
Bringing the Light into each village, each tribe, each Ruler
Uniting, soothing, and quelling discord.

(Pause)

Merlin:
And from each place in the land come invisible messengers
Bringing their needs and desires.
To be refreshed by the power of the Dragons
And the need fire of the Ather.

To these we give the blessing of the Mather, the Ather and Amhran.

Merlin raises arms in the Position of Creation and then crashes bracelets together and then sings:

*OOOOOOOOOOOOOOOOOOOOOOOOOOOOOO
UUUUUUUUUUUUUUUUUUUUUUUUUUUUUU
EEEEEEEEEEEEEEEEEEEEEEEEEEEEEEEE*

As he sings OOOOOOOO so does the White Pendragon sing OOOOOOOO. When he sings UUUUUUUUUU likewise does the Red Pendragon sings UUUUUUUUUUUUUUUUUU and when EEEEEEEEEEEEE Amhran sings EEEEEEEEEEEEEE.

Spring Equinox

Merlin: *The sun's rays warm the land and the days have grown long.*

Amhran (starts to play scales): *The shoots are unfolding in the sacred groves and blossoms carpet the forrest floor.*

Merlin: *I am in the growth of the plants, the light that shimmers on water, in the smile of a child, in the tears of an old man, in the bee on the flower, in the rutting of deer, in the clash of swords, in the love of man and woman. I dance in the world of creation*

Amhran: *I play the dance of the quickening months.*

White Pendragon: *The song plays summer's dance. The sun's fires are stoked and the warm winds of the South run across the land.*

Red Pendragon: *The Tree's blossoms are transformed into a verdant carpet and the Oinacos lives.*

Amhran: *The song is one of life, the Emerald Heart of the World's heartbeat, of the seeds of meditation growing into trees of revelation.*

Merlin: *Yet in this dance, I put aside all the meditations of the old man and live for each second of sunlight, each smile of a lover, each swing of the sword, each sunrise and sun set. Now is not the moment to understand, now is the time to watch plants reaching for the Ather, for the birth of the babes born in the womb of the mother.*

> *There are times of doing and undoing*
> *Of Acting and Thinking*
> *Now is the time to take to the plough*
> *Go to war*
> *And to take actions.*

Amhran: *The Oinacos has spoken, let the Song of the Equinox begin.*

Merlin raises arms in the Position of Creation and then crashes bracelets together and then sings:

OOOOOOOOOOOOOOOOOOOOOOOOOOOOOO
UUUUUUUUUUUUUUUUUUUUUUUUUUUUUU
EEEEEEEEEEEEEEEEEEEEEEEEEEEEEEEE

As he sings OOOOOOOO so does the White Pendragon sing OOOOOOOO. When he sings UUUUUUUUUUU likewise does the Red Pendragon sings UUUUUUUUUUUUUUUUUU and when EEEEEEEEEEEEE Amhran sings EEEEEEEEEEEEEE.

Winter Solstice

Merlin: *The sun hath reached its lowest point and has no power upon the land.*

Amhran (starts to play slow scales): *The land is barren, frozen and cold. The winter's store is half empty and men grow weary of old food.*

Merlin: *The seed of my knowledge sleeps in the cold still earth. It is the fruit of my contemplation of the previous year. Yet if it receives not the warmth of the sun of new experience it shall rot. I seek experience again, knowledge of myself in creation.*

Amhran: *I halt the song (stops playing scales) so that the seed may quicken and the Oinacos may be born anew in creation.*

White Pendragon: *The song has stopped. The sun awakes with a new energy and stokes his fire and to increase its position in the heights of the heavens. The wind starts to warm.*

Red Pendragon: *The dead trees start to bud with life and the seeds of the Oinacos's experience sprout into a new beginning.*

Amhran: *A new song begins* (starts playing scales faster): *one of action, where all things turn from within to without.*

White Pendragon: *The winds of the world blow warmer, the fires of the sun replace the fires of the hearth.*

Red Pendragon: *The waters of the world are warmed and become the delight of the spring rain. The rocks warm to the gentle sun.*

Merlin: In this warmth I start to experience the Life of the Song.
I am a tree reaching to heaven, I am the faun in the glen, the birds in the air, I am the child at play, the farmer at his planting, the woman in labour, the warriors at war, I am the King on his throne.
I have the eyes of a hawk
The ears of a hare
The tongue of a snake
The nose of a hound
The touch of a lover's caress
To cleave unto every part of creation.
To know and to see my own reflection.
There are times of doing and undoing
Of Acting and Thinking
Now is the time to plough
To war
And To Act.

Amhran: *The Oinacos has spoken, let the Song of the Solstice begin.*

Merlin raises arms in the Position of Creation and then crashes bracelets together and then sings:

OOOOOOOOOOOOOOOOOOOOOOOOOOOOOOO
UUUUUUUUUUUUUUUUUUUUUUUUUUUUUUU
EEEEEEEEEEEEEEEEEEEEEEEEEEEEEEEEEEE

As he sings OOOOOOOO so does the White Pendragon sing OOOOOOOO. When he sings UUUUUUUUUU likewise does the Red Pendragon sings UUUUUUUUUUUUUUUUU and when EEEEEEEEEEEEE Amhran sings EEEEEEEEEEEEEE.

Other Titles from Thoth Publications:

THE GRAIL SEEKER'S COMPANION
By John Matthews & Marian Green

There have been many books about the Grail, written from many differing standpoints. Some have been practical, some purely historical, others literary, but this is the first Grail book which sets out to help the esoterically inclined seeker through the maze of symbolism, character and myth which surrounds the central point of the Grail.

In today's frantic world when many people have their material needs met some still seek spiritual fulfilment. They are drawn to explore the old philosophies and traditions, particularly that of our Western Celtic Heritage. It is here they encounter the quest for the Holy Grail, that mysterious object which will bring hope and healing to all. Some have come to recognise that they dwell in a spiritual wasteland and now search that symbol of the grail which may be the only remedy. Here is the guide book for the modern seeker, explaining the history and pointing clearly towards the Aquarian grail of the future.

John Matthews and Marian Green have each been involved in the study of the mysteries of Britain and the Grail myth for over thirty-five years. In THE GRAIL SEEKER'S COMPANION they have provided a guidebook not just to places, but to people, stories and theories surrounding the Grail. A reference book of Grail-ology, including history, ritual, meditation, advice and instruction. In short, everything you are likely to need before you set out on the most important adventure of your life.

This is the only book that points the way to the Holy Grail Quest in the 21st. century.

ISBN 1 870450 49 3

APPRENTICED TO MAGIC
By W.E.Butler

This volume is for the true aspirant after magical attainment. In his earlier books the author has defined the real magical art and described the training to be undergone by the serious student. Now he goes a step further, and has written a book which, if properly read, meditated upon, and followed up, will bring those who are ready to the doors of the Mysteries.

This book is not for those who seek sensation. It has been written by one who has himself followed the magical path as a sound and competent guide for all who seek initiation into the Western Mysteries.

Contents include:

Application Accepted
First Exercises
Postures and Breathing
Meditation
The Tree of Life
The Tree as an Indicator
The Contact of Power
Bring Through the Power
The Gates are Open

ISBN 1-870450-41-8

PRACTICAL MAGIC AND THE WESTERN MYSTERY TRADITION
Unpublished Essays and Articles by W. E. Butler.

W. E. Butler, a devoted friend and colleague of the celebrated occultist Dion Fortune, was among those who helped build the Society of the Inner Light into the foremost Mystery School of its day. He then went on to found his own school, the Servants of the Light, which still continues under the guidance of Dolores Ashcroft-Nowicki, herself an occultist and author of note and the editor and compiler of this volume.

PRACTICAL MAGIC AND THE WESTERN TRADITION is a collection of previously unpublished articles, training papers, and lectures covering many aspects of practical magic in the context of western occultism that show W. E. Butler not only as a leading figure in the magical tradition of the West, but also as one of its greatest teachers.

Subjects covered include:

What makes an Occultist
Ritual Training
Inner Plane Contacts and Rays
The Witch Cult
Keys in Practical Magic
Telesmatic Images
Words of Power
An Explanation of Some Psychic Phenomena

ISBN 1-870450-32-9

www.ingramcontent.com/pod-product-compliance
Lightning Source LLC
Chambersburg PA
CBHW040226180426
43200CB00026BA/2941